The Fight for Joy

Reflections on the Book of Philippians

Jason M. Garwood

ISBN: 1481039601
ISBN-13: 978-1481039604

DEDICATION

To my beautiful wife Mary.
Thank you for always loving me.
May God's grace continue to be evident in our lives.

To my children: Elijah, Avery, and Nathan.
You are a precious gift to us and your God is amazing.
My prayer is that joy will be the central
characteristic of your life as you follow Him.

CONTENTS

Acknowledgments   i

1 Introduction   1

2 While Alone   19

3 When Suffering   43

4 Facing Death   65

5 With Humility   85

6 In the World, With Others   101

7 With Christ's Righteousness   123

8 When You Are Tired   143

9 As We Wait   161

10 When Anxious   179

11 Being Content Without Riches   201

ACKNOWLEDGMENTS

I want to thank my family for always being a source of joy; the church I have been entrusted to, for loving Jesus and fighting for joy; my staff for always extending grace to me; Josh Whipple, Sherri Hoy, Julie Priestley and Lane Walker for taking the time to read this and offer some critique and encouragement; my brother, Brett and Red Bag Media for the amazing cover design; and Jesus, "Who *for the joy set before him endured the cross*, despising the shame, and is seated at the right hand of the throne of God" (Hebrews 12:2).

i

1 - INTRODUCTION

Paul and Timothy, servants of Christ Jesus, to all the saints in Christ Jesus who are at Philippi, with the overseers and deacons: Grace to you and peace from God our Father and the Lord Jesus Christ.[1]

The book you are holding is the outworking of a thirteen-week sermon series I preached in the winter of 2012-2013.[2] I have always loved the book of Philippians—such artistry, imagination, passion and profound language. It contains only four chapters, one hundred and four verses, and is well worth the fifteen minutes or so it takes to read it. In fact, it might be helpful to go and read the entire letter before diving

---

[1] Philippians 1:1-2 (ESV). Scripture quotations are from The Holy Bible, English Standard Version® (ESV®), copyright © 2001 by Crossway, a publishing ministry of Good News Publishers. Used by permission. All rights reserved.

[2] For podcast information, please visit www.colwood.org.

into this book.

My aim in undertaking this project is fairly straightforward (yet paradoxically, it is an incredibly difficult task). I hope to edify you by exalting the glory of God that shines so brightly in the face of Jesus Christ. This demands so much of us for it requires that we see sin as being bitter and Christ as being sweet. It demands above everything else that we see Jesus and his glorious gospel as being the highest treasure we could ever desire. In short, it requires us to see and savor the beauty of God demonstrated in the person and work of Jesus Christ, the Son of God.[3]

The curious thing about the book of Philippians is both its doctrinal depth and simplicity in message. Paul conveys several deep theological truths in just a short amount of time, and he does so in a concise manner. While there are plenty of well-known verses that people like to memorize, we should keep in mind what is central to Paul's theology: the crucified and risen Messiah. This is the vision behind the book. Christ is everything to the apostle. *Philippians is all about Jesus.*

On an editorial note, I have taken Paul's thought process and uniquely outlined it. There are eleven chapters to this treatise, and while there are several ways to outline Philippians, I have chosen to stick closely with how I preached the book both exegetically

---

[3] May we never forget the beautiful promise of Scripture: "You make known to me the path of life; in your presence there is *fullness of joy*; at your right hand are pleasures forevermore" (Psalm 16:11), emphasis mine.

and thematically.

As a brief preface, please know that I have prayed for you. As I type this, I've asked the Triune God to bless your efforts in reading something that will eventually fade into the memory several years from now (there is something incredibly human about a project like this!). I have asked the Spirit to bring conviction and joy to you as you journey with me. May God himself, the only source of infinite joy, be exalted and honored as you read.

THE STORY BEFORE THE STORY

The book of Philippians starts in Acts 16. It is there the Apostle Paul journeys into Roman territory to preach a gospel about a new king that has arrived—and this is, of course, offensive to Caesar himself. *Jesus is Lord* is that gospel.[4] The implication then? Jesus is Lord, *not* Caesar. Such a message is worthy of the death penalty—something Paul faced circa 64-67 A.D.

The book of Acts, outlined by Luke the doctor, chronicles the journey of the apostle and his Spirit-anointed preaching and church planting throughout the known world.

In chapter 1 of Acts, Jesus ascends back to the Father to inherit his Kingdom.[5] Afterwards, the disciples are sent back to Jerusalem to await further instructions.

Chapter 2 of Acts contains a unique story of the Holy

---

[4] Phil. 1:2, 14; 2:11, 19, 24, 29; 3:1, 8, 20; 4:1-2, 4-5, 10, 23.

[5] Acts 1:6-11; cf. Daniel 7:13-14.

Spirit falling upon Jesus' followers and Peter, in response to this incredible event, steps up to preach the greatest sermon ever uttered. From there, the church explodes in growth as many Jews repent and believe in Messiah.

In chapter 7 of Acts, something changes, however. Stephen is the first Christian martyr and verse one of chapter eight says "Saul approved of his execution." Saul.[6] This is the first we've heard of this man, and he approved of Stephen's execution.

The brilliant writer, Luke, intends for us to continue to read on in order to find out more about this man. Luke says that Saul was "ravaging the church" and sending Christians to prison (8:3). This man is decidedly against this small Jewish sect making any sort advancement within Judaism, and he intends to stop it at all cost.

Luke finishes chapter 8 with three positive stories and is quick to remind us that Saul is still "breathing threats and murder against the disciples of the Lord" (9:1).

Everything changes at this point, however. Saul heads north to Damascus to continue his violent agenda when suddenly Jesus appears and knocks him off of his high horse.

Jesus asks why Saul is persecuting him and tells him

---

[6] Saul is a Jewish name. As he goes about his business in the book of Acts, his name will be "changed" to Paul. This is his Roman name, so he didn't necessarily change it, but simply uses Paul to leverage his influence in the Roman Empire as a citizen with certain privileges.

to go into the city and await further instructions.

Following this, Jesus appears to Ananias and instructs him to go and meet with Saul in order to restore Saul's vision. Ananias is reluctant to want to do this because he has heard all about Saul and his hostile temper. Jesus then replies to Ananias with something unbelievable.

> Go, for he is a chosen instrument of mine to carry my name before the Gentiles and kings and the children of Israel. For *I will show him how much he must suffer* for the sake of my name.[7]

This is one of the most weighty verses in all of Scripture. Set aside for a moment the mystery of the doctrine of predestination. Set aside for a moment the question of election and how God works in his choosing of those to whom he will extend his grace. Set aside for a moment the complexities of the story, and be utterly devastated by this statement. Be blown away by Jesus' remarks.

Jesus has "chosen" (his words) Saul to exult the name of Christ to *everyone*. Gentiles, kings and Israelites: all are to be made aware, by Saul that Jesus is Lord. However, Jesus does not stop there. At this point, the task seems incredibly glorifying, easy, and straightforward. Think about it; Saul could have meekly responded at this point, "Great, Jesus. I did not realize it was you that I was persecuting, but I'm glad we had this discussion. I will go joyfully from here and tell people about you."

---

[7] Acts 9:15-16, emphasis mine.

To the contrary, this is not what happens in the story. Jesus attaches something to the task. The task is not simply the preaching of the gospel to the nations, though this is certainly a noteworthy part of it. He carries with the task an ethic. The ethic is *suffering*. "I will show [you] how much [you] must suffer for the sake of my name." This is nothing short than astonishing to me.

Apparently, in Jesus' eyes, suffering is a significant part of this world and in order to redeem the world to its original design sans sin, *suffering must be leveraged for the sake of the gospel.* Let us never forget that the very content of the gospel is the *crucified* Messiah. Suffering is an ethic of the Kingdom of God and a theology of the cross[8] is central to it.

All of this is vital to keep in mind as the story of the Philippian church unfolds.

THE CHURCH IS PLANTED

Back to Acts 16. Paul is traveling on his second missionary journey,[9] and while he is traveling, the Holy Spirit forbids the group to go to Asia. From the region of Phrygia and Galatia they travel northwest towards Bithynia, but the Spirit of Jesus forbids them to go there, too. So Paul, Timothy and Silas head to Troas and while

---

[8] More on the "theology of the cross" in Chapter 2.

[9] Students of the Bible often organize the book of Acts by classifying Paul's trips in numerical order. Traditionally, Paul goes on (at least) three different journeys and most people accept this as being historically accurate when reading Acts.

there, a man "in the night" asks him to come to Macedonia to help them (16:9). As soon as the vision was over, the group joins up with Luke and heads that way "concluding that God had called [them] to preach the gospel" to the Macedonian people (16:10).[10]

Having left Troas, they made it to Neapolis and from there ventured ten miles to Philippi.

The city of Philippi (located on the Egnatian Way–a popular trade route for the region built in second-century B.C.) was named after Alexander the Great's father, Philip of Macedon in 356 B.C. Following the dismantling of the Grecian empire, it came under Roman control in 168 B.C. Later on, the city was retaken when Antony and Octavian (the would-be Augustus Caesar) defeated Brutus and Cassius (the assassins of Julies Caesar) there in 42 B.C.[11] Many soldiers made Philippi their home after the battle(s) and years to follow, so the Greek-speaking town became influenced by the Latin language as the city's culture shifted to all things Roman. (It is beneficial to take note that Paul tells the Philippians that their citizenship is in heaven and that Jesus is Lord. This message is in direct contradiction to the fact that the residents there held a citizenship in Rome and believed Caesar, the emperor, to be lord.)

When Paul and his companions arrive to Philippi,

---

[10] It is crucial to note that the pronoun "we" is used here in verse 10 because Luke joins the group and since Luke is writing the book of Acts, he can interject himself into the story.

[11] Frank Thielman, *Philippians*. The NIV Application Commentary (Grand Rapids, MI: Zondervan Publishing House, 1995), 16.

they stay in the city for several days. As was his normal custom, Paul searched for a synagogue to preach in, but apparently did not find one. As the Jewish Sabbath rolls around, the group goes outside of the city gate to the river, believing there to be a place to pray. In doing so, they were hoping to find some Jewish friends.[12] While several women were present, the first one they talk with is a woman named Lydia.

Lydia was from Thyatira and Luke (paying attention to detail as usual) tells us that she was a seller of purple goods and a worshiper of the God of Israel. In other words, she is rich and loves Yahweh. This is the start of Paul's core team in his church plant. Luke says that the Lord "opened her heart" as Paul preached the gospel to the group (16:14). Lydia and her family repented, and were baptized. Her first act of Christian faith is an act of hospitality, as she hosts Paul and friends in her home.

As Paul and company are on their way to prayer, a slave girl and her owners follow them. Not only does she follow Paul, she tells everyone listening that he and his group are "servants of the Most High God...who proclaim to you the way of salvation" (16:17). For those of Greek background, the most high god of Grecian religion was Zeus.

Several days later Paul, seizing the opportunity,

---

[12] Jewish law required that there be ten Jewish men in a city in order to form a synagogue. Given what Luke tells us, there may not have been ten there in the city. Paul (being a former Pharisee) knows that on the Sabbath he might find some law-abiding Jews by the river, as many would be there for ceremonial washings and prayer.

commands the demon to come out, and it does so. The slave girl's owners are irate and take Paul and Silas to the magistrates to have them thrown in prison for disrupting their Roman practices. A reaction from the crowd ensues, and the two men are beaten and thrown in jail.

At around midnight, as Paul and Silas are singing to God, an earthquake hits and the shackles open, along with the doors. The jailer wakes up from his slumber and rather than face death at the hands of his superiors for his insubordination and obvious mess-up, he draws his sword to kill himself. Paul stops the man in time and lets him know that they are still inside. The man asks Paul how he is going to get out of this mess and Paul tells him to believe in Jesus the true Lord of the world. The jailer repents and believes (as does his entire household, a notable pattern in Acts) and in God's providence, the magistrates let them all go. Leveraging his Roman citizenship, Paul demands that the officials come and speak with him first, so that they know that this situation is a gross violation of Roman law. After the magistrates and police find out that they were Roman citizens, they took them out and sent them on their way. Paul and Silas reconvene with the group and meet up with Lydia. After some time, they leave and head to the next city.

A rich woman, slave girl, Roman guard, and their families are the first group of misfits to be a part of the church at Philippi. It is a messy beginning, but the gospel brings messy people to completion through salvation in Jesus. This is the story of the church at

Philippi.

THE BEGINNING OF THE FIGHT FOR JOY

Of all the doctrinal matters that have changed my life, it is *Christian Hedonism* that has impacted me the most. John Piper[13] has dedicated his life to this all-important belief: "God is most glorified in us when we are most satisfied in him."[14]

The implications of this are huge. The beloved doctrine says that the greatest way you can give weight and honor to God (glorify) is by treasuring in, delighting in, and finding ultimate satisfaction in God. The mind, will, and emotions, when captivated by the beauty of God, find satisfaction in the Infinite. Rather than finding satisfaction in idols (which over-promise and under-deliver), we are commanded to fight for joy *in God*. This is how God can be given the most glory: by fighting for joy. Jared Wilson writes:

> Joy is an implication of the gospel, but is not implied for the Christian life—it is commanded. It is not optional... Joy is deeper than happiness, but like happiness, joy is always circumstantial. Because the gospel is true, then, even when we aren't happy we can know the deeper joy

---

[13] John Piper is the former pastor for preaching and vision at Bethlehem Baptist Church in Minneapolis, Minnesota. He has written dozens of books that all deal with this incredible, Bible-saturated, historically attested to belief of Christian Hedonism. For more information, visit www.desiringgod.org.

[14] John Piper, *The Dangerous Duty of Delight* (Sisters, OR: Multnomah, 2001), 20.

because of the circumstances of God's goodness and love. On the permanent condition of God's unrelenting grace, joy is a permanent possibility... Indeed, not to rejoice is sin.[15]

We will look more closely at this in the ensuing chapters.

Consequently, the gospel is now the avenue by which we come to faith *and* grow in faith. In a nutshell, the gospel is that from birth, we are dead in our sins, utterly helpless and unable to make ourselves friends of God; however, God has miraculously intervened in the person of Jesus, not only to atone for our sins perfectly, but also to grant us his righteousness, fully justifying you and me before God. This means that when the Father looks upon us, it is as though we have never sinned and as though we have always obeyed. We are far more sinful than we will ever admit, yet far more loved than we could ever dare imagine. And it all rests on the shoulders of our great God and Savior, Jesus Christ. It is upon Jesus' obedience that we bank our joy on because a Holy, Wrathful, Patient and Loving God of Justice gives us his righteousness as a gift.

THE BOOK OF PHILIPPIANS

The apostle Paul writes this letter from prison in Rome, in the year 60 A.D., as a response to the sending of Epaphroditus with a gift from Paul's first church on

---

[15] Jared C. Wilson, *Gospel Deeps* (Wheaton, IL: Crossway Books, 2012), 82-84.

European soil. Not only is he writing to thank them for their generosity, he sends them some further instructions and encouragement, too. Paul's encouragement is centered on the gospel with the task of fighting for joy.

If anyone had reason to murmur with ingratitude, it was Paul:

> I am talking like a madman—with far greater labors, far more imprisonments, with countless beatings, and often near death. Five times I received at the hands of the Jews the forty lashes less one. Three times I was beaten with rods. Once I was stoned. Three times I was shipwrecked; a night and a day I was adrift at sea; on frequent journeys, in danger from rivers, danger from robbers, danger from my own people, danger from Gentiles, danger in the city, danger in the wilderness, danger at sea, danger from false brothers; in toil and hardship, through many a sleepless night, in hunger and thirst, often without food, in cold and exposure. And, apart from other things, there is the daily pressure on me of my anxiety for all the churches.[16]

When Jesus said that Paul was going to suffer for the cause of the gospel and Jesus' name, he undoubtedly meant it—and Paul certainly went through it. What is true is that Paul suffered. What is also true is that Paul fought for joy despite circumstances which would utterly dumbfound us as Christians living in the

---

[16] 2 Corinthians 11:23b-28.

comforts of the Western world. If anyone had the circumstances in which to curse God, it was Paul; yet through this, the Spirit kept him close to the gospel, reminding Paul of his identity as a servant of Jesus (Phil. 1:1).

In the book of Philippians, Paul uses "joy," "rejoice," or some form of the word sixteen times. On each and every page of this letter we can find joy. The basic thread throughout the book rests upon three crucial things: (1) God is sovereign; (2) the gospel is central, and (3) the New Creation is our home. When Paul situates joy within the text, it is almost always related to the objective reality of Christ's person and work. For Paul, the fight for joy begins with the indicative reality of the gospel and flows out from there in an imperative (command) to respond a certain way *based upon the truth of the gospel.* James Montgomery Boice writes, "the name of "Christ" or "Jesus Christ" occurs seventeen times in the first chapter alone," demonstrating that Paul is acutely aware of whom he owes his life to and whom it is he worships.[17]

What is curious about this letter, too, is how Paul uses some reference to the mind sixteen times. The mind is a grand-central station for how our emotions, affections and actions function. The battlefield is in the mind and what we choose to believe about God. Either we will believe the truth about God, or we will exchange it for a lie (Rom. 1:25). The secret to fighting for joy can

---

[17] James Montgomery Boice, *Philippians: An Expositional Commentary* (Grand Rapids, MI: Baker Books, 2000), 13.

be found in what we think and trust.

Philippians is unlike several of the other letters of Paul that we find in the New Testament. For example, Paul does not spend an extraordinary amount of time correcting problems as he does in 1 and 2 Corinthians—though he does ask Euodia and Syntyche to agree in the Lord (4:2). He also does not spend a lot of time exhausting the riches of the glorious truths behind God's electing grace as he does in Ephesians. He doesn't talk about marriage (Eph., 1 Cor.) or even offer advice on being a pastor (1 and 2 Timothy, Titus). The tone is different.

Considered a "friendship letter," Philippians is a style of writing which was immensely popular and taken seriously in the ancient world.[18] The church at Philippi is remarkably close to Paul's heart and given the story previously laid out, one can imagine why this is the case.

Many have come to love this short letter for many different reasons. Personally, it is one of my favorite books, though I tend to have a hard time picking only one. The book speaks of ways we can be generous, maintain unity in the church, find joy instead of worry, make peace instead of disunity, live with courage and boldness, and lean on the truth of the gospel.

At its core, Philippians hinges on the truth of the humiliation and exaltation of Jesus found in 2:5-11. Everything revolves around this great passage as Christ provides for us the example of how to live. From

---

[18] See discussion in Gordon D. Fee, *Paul's Letter to the Philippians* (Grand Rapids, MI: W.B Eerdmans Pub. Co., 1995), 2.

beginning to end, the gospel is the focus and our subsequent participation (*koinonia*) in it.

THE TEXT

Paul opens up with a standard greeting by saying hello to his cherished friends. He loves them, cares for them and wants them to know about it. He lets them know that Timothy is with him and that there is much community and love between all of them.

Unlike other letters where Paul refers to himself as an apostle, he calls himself (and Timothy) *servants*.[19] This is not by accident. He has served the church well. Apparently Paul's apostleship is not in question as it had been in other letters. His relationship and authority as an apostle of Jesus Christ is known and assumed, speaking volumes to the assertion that the two had a thriving relationship. Knowing what is to come in chapter 2 as it relates to Jesus and him becoming a servant *for* us, Paul can only be reminded that he is a servant by virtue of Jesus serving him first.[20]

Following this, Paul greets the "saints" *in* Christ Jesus "with the overseers and deacons" (1:1). The word "saints" (*hagios*) implies holiness and set apartness. The

---

[19] Fee writes, "For the (basically Gentile) readers of this letter, this word would have only meant "slave." Indeed, *douloi* were so common in Greco-Roman society that no one would have thought it to refer other than to those owned by, and subservient to, the master of a household." Ibid., 62-63.

[20] Matthew 20:28, "...even as the Son of Man came not to be served but to serve."

Philippian church has been consecrated *to* God. Not only this, the church is set apart *for* God's purposes, too. Paul is quick to connect this derived holiness to Jesus as they are "in" him, implying that holiness cannot be achieved apart from the saving righteousness and grace of Jesus that he gives to the sinner by grace alone.

The word "overseer" is translated as "bishop," but it is more like what we would think of as an elder, the leaders in a local church. The word "deacon" implies those who lead the church by serving, oftentimes providing people in need with food and healthcare. Here, Paul acknowledges the local leadership and their duty of mutual service.

Paul then goes on to say "grace to you and peace from God our Father and the Lord Jesus Christ," to the beloved church (1:2).

IT'S ALL ABOUT JESUS

Grace and peace are commanding words. Grace is oftentimes explained as the "unmerited favor of God." Peace (*shalom*) is the result of said grace, as God works to restore our relationship that had been previously marked by hostility.

These words are often overlooked at the beginning of Paul's letters. They are explosive words jam packed with meaning. Let's start with grace.

The problem with defining grace as the unmerited favor of God is that it leaves out a central component: Jesus. Here's what I mean.

If you were to walk up to someone and tell them that God loves them, would you be accurate? Yes, and no.

Surely God loves them in the sense that he loves the world, his creation (Jn. 3:16) and has a favorable disposition towards it; but God's love and justice are never at odds. The Bible says that God hates sinners (Psalm 5:5). God's love is not a cheap flighty feeling—as though he could set aside our sin for a few moments and lavish upon us a few niceties of sorts. He does not love at the expense of his justice. So yes, you would be accurate, but no you would not be.

Is grace unmerited? Absolutely. There is no question about it. When God saves a sinner, he does so by regenerating his/her heart and granting the Holy Spirit to prompt faith in a person's life. You cannot earn this. Dead people do not wake themselves up to receive a gift, regardless of how free it is. Their heart must be resurrected by the Spirit, *first*. This grace, however, cannot be given to someone outside the bounds of the person and work of Jesus. It is through Jesus alone. If you wanted to be more accurate in the above scenario, you would have to speak of the gospel.

The unmerited favor, which is bestowed on an individual, is conditional, and that condition is the gospel. This is the reason Paul says that grace and peace are *from* God the Father and the Lord Jesus Christ. That is to say, the Father and the Son are responsible for the church's existence, and because of Jesus' work, he grants their new identity in the present. Those who are united in Christ are united with him in an inseparable union. This cannot happen outside of God's work in the gospel.

Because of this grace, peace is the result. No longer does the wrath of God abide on the Christian's head.

Christ's propitiatory sacrifice has removed this wrath and judgment because Jesus has taken it on himself in our place. Because of his substitutionary death, peace with God is now possible. Consequently, we are now able to join in on the New Creation project, all because of the cross.

Paul opens up his letter of joy by carefully explaining some of the most fundamental truths found in the gospel. He begins by reminding us that it's all about Jesus. He is the hero and savior; let us be reminded of this again and again. This is the background and beginning to the letter. Now we continue the fight for joy.

2 - WHILE ALONE

I thank my God in all my remembrance of you, always in every prayer of mine for you all making my prayer with joy, because of your partnership in the gospel from the first day until now. And I am sure of this, that he who began a good work in you will bring it to completion at the day of Jesus Christ. It is right for me to feel this way about you all, because I hold you in my heart, for you are all partakers with me of grace, both in my imprisonment and in the defense and confirmation of the gospel. For God is my witness, how I yearn for you all with the affection of Christ Jesus. And it is my prayer that your love may abound more and more, with knowledge and all discernment, so that you may approve what is excellent, and so be pure and blameless for the day of Christ, filled with the fruit of righteousness that comes through Jesus Christ, to the glory and praise of God.[1]

---

[1] Phil. 1:3-11.

When I say "fight" for joy, I intend to mean several things that have several connotations and assumptions. To start, we are commanded to fight the good fight of faith (1 Tim. 6:12). By implication, this means that there are things that we fight for and other things we fight against. When we fight for joy, we are fighting against unbelief, ingratitude, depression, complaining, murmuring, idolatry, anxiety, and the various fruits of sin we promulgate in the flesh. *Against* these things we ought to fight.

The things we fight *for* are the truths about God and us, things that sin tends to distort. At its root, the fight for joy is a fight to believe God. If we grant the premise that God is the infinite source of joy (Ps. 16:11, 43:40), then it follows that your fight is a fight to get God. It is a journey of discovery as we learn more about whom God is in the person and work of Jesus. John Piper helps connect this for us:

> Faith is something that must be fought for, if it is to thrive and survive. This is how we take hold on eternal life—by fighting to maintain faith, with its joy in Christ.[2]

THE ROOT OF LONELINESS
To be sure, loneliness is deep-seated in sin. Genesis 1-2 discloses the creation story for us. The Creator God makes all things through the power of his word. Being of

---

[2] John Piper, *When I Don't Desire God: How to Fight for Joy* (Wheaton, IL: Crossway Books, 2004), 37.

true free and ultimate will, God decides to create *ex nihilo* (out of nothing) as an expression of his love and grace. He does not create because he is insecure, bored or even lonely—for God is Triune, and the Father, Son and Spirit share an eternal bond of mutual submission, self-sacrifice and glory. God creates in order to extend the love that exists within himself to his creation by shaping it and molding it as "good."

What is curious about the creation story is the fact that everything is good except one thing. The light, darkness, animals, water and land are reckoned as good and right. The first human creature Adam, however, is alone and this is not good and not right (Gen. 2:18). Part of God's plan for humans is not only the cultivation of the land, but also the blessing to be fruitful and increase it. In other words, humans are to make and create culture through procreation and hard work. But Adam cannot do this alone; he needs a helper fit for him.

According to this remarkable story, loneliness characterized Adam's condition *before* sin; however, after sin enters into the souls of the couple, and subsequently the world, the two experience loneliness to an even higher degree.

When Genesis 3 comes about, the serpent leads Eve into temptation, and her lustful eyes engage in iniquity. Standing quietly near the exchange, Adam fell into sin with Eve by consuming the forbidden fruit. Instantaneously, they are ashamed and realize that they are naked (3:7). The implication of this story, then, is that nakedness brings shame instead of glory, and it must be covered up. Loneliness is now the new reality in which the two must walk.

At the end of chapter 3, "[God] drove out the man, and at the east of the garden of Eden he placed the cherubim and a flaming sword that turned every way to guard the way to the tree of life" (vs. 24). Having been expelled from their glorious position of prominence, Adam and Eve now struggle under creation instead of ruling over it (3:18). They are no longer able to be kept inside the garden because their sin has now become a stench to God (Is. 65:5). A Holy God cannot be in fellowship with sinful man—not without mediation.

The issue with sin, at its root, is ungodliness. It is a failure to live up to the perfect standard of righteousness that is God himself. Since we are disassociated from God because of sin, we are unable to have genuine fellowship with him. Paul describes this condition elsewhere as being, "dead in [our] trespasses and sins" (Eph. 2:1). Many people have said that pride is the root of all sin, but I believe it is ungodliness. Sin is not simply an issue of the will (like making a willful decision to do something immoral), but is a condition we are enslaved within (Ro. 6:17). The concern here is the doctrine of total depravity. Sin pollutes us throughout every faculty of our being, and consequently, we are utterly helpless to save ourselves. We are not as bad as we could be—thanks to God's grace—but we are corrupt at the very core of our nature. The stench of sin blemishes every part of us. Our image bearing qualities have become distorted, and our moral will bent towards sin.

Because of this condition, we are lonely (e.g., Lev.

13:46). We are isolated reprobates who have the wrath of God on our collective head (Eph. 2:3, cf. Ro. 5:19). We deserve nothing short of eternity in darkness. Alone. Because of our sin. In Adam all die.

I am aware that this is a fairly unwelcoming picture to describe. I do not want you to miss the glories of the gospel message that can restore this broken relationship. But please do not gloss over this reality as though we ought to not to talk about our sin. God is disgusted with our contraventions, so let us think soberly about them (Ps. 5:5, 1 Cor. 15:22).

This is the root of our loneliness.

Have you ever felt alone, feeling as if no one cares? Have you ever felt abandoned by someone; maybe even someone you considered a best friend? Do you stand in the middle of the crowd and still feel as though you are the only one there? If this is you, understand that this is not the goal of God. The fight for joy while alone begins when you understand that God's vision for a new heaven and a new earth includes the restoration of your loneliness. Your feeling of loneliness is not the final word. Sin is never the final word. Jesus is.

Now that we have this out of the way, it is time to take a look at our culture and how loneliness has truly become an epidemic.

THE REALITY OF LONELINESS

Though we may never admit it, we are becoming increasingly lonely as a society. Several of us hide behind our Twitter and Facebook accounts, hoping to exert influence without committing to someone for fear of a dozen different things. We are able to "stay connected" while sitting alone behind the computer screen or iPhone. The world is superficially shrinking, too. We can communicate with someone across the world in a matter of seconds while simultaneously feeling entirely isolated. It is a bizarre thought to contemplate, but things are certainly changing.

I recently stumbled upon a couple of articles that speak to this issue of loneliness. One of them said:

> We are living in an isolation that would have been unimaginable to our ancestors, and yet we have never been more accessible. Over the past three decades, technology has delivered to us a world in which we need not be out of contact for a fraction of a moment. In 2010, at a cost of $300 million, 800 miles of fiber-optic cable was laid between the Chicago Mercantile Exchange and the New York Stock Exchange to shave three milliseconds off trading times. Yet within this world of instant and absolute communication, unbounded by limits of time or space, we suffer from unprecedented alienation. We have never been more detached from one another, or lonelier. In a world consumed by ever more novel modes of socializing, we have less and less actual society. We live in an accelerating contradiction: the more connected we become, the lonelier we are. We were promised a global village; instead we inhabit the drab cul-de-sacs and endless freeways of a vast suburb of information.[3]

---

[3] "Is Facebook Making Us Lonely?" *The Atlantic* (May, 2012), http://www.theatlantic.com/magazine/archive/2012/05/is-facebook-making-us-lonely/308930/.

And a cul-de-sac it truly is! Never before have we been so connected as humans in our communication; yet the issue of loneliness is still a growing concern.

The article goes on to say that:

> We know intuitively that loneliness and being alone are not the same thing. Solitude can be lovely. Crowded parties can be agony. We also know, thanks to a growing body of research on the topic, that loneliness is not a matter of external conditions; it is a psychological state. A 2005 analysis of data from a longitudinal study of Dutch twins showed that the tendency toward loneliness has roughly the same genetic component as other psychological problems such as neuroticism or anxiety.[4]

What is obvious is that proximity and affinity are not the central concerns for loneliness, but rather psychology and our perception of the world. In other words, just because we are near or far from people physically will not change how we feel, nor does it matter what we have in common with someone. You could be busy at work in a cubicle surrounded by hundreds of other workers and while participating in the daily flow of office work, feel entirely alone, maybe feeling inadequate, insecure, and depressed.

The fact of the matter is that loneliness includes a horde of other emotions, too. Depression is a serious

---

[4] Ibid.

issue—one that is proven by the fact that prescription drug sales are at an all-time high in our country. With the recent focus on bullying at school, it follows logically that insecurity and inadequacies are also affecting our children. Contrary to what you may feel regarding this matter, social interaction does matter:

> Loneliness and being alone are not the same thing, but both are on the rise. We meet fewer people. We gather less. And when we gather, our bonds are less meaningful and less easy. The decrease in confidants—that is, in quality social connections—has been dramatic over the past 25 years. In one survey, the mean size of networks of personal confidants decreased from 2.94 people in 1985 to 2.08 in 2004. Similarly, in 1985, only 10 percent of Americans said they had no one with whom to discuss important matters, and 15 percent said they had only one such good friend. By 2004, 25 percent had nobody to talk to, and 20 percent had only one confidant.[5]

What's at stake here is the very meaning behind what it means to be human. Biblically, we are to be a connected people. But according to recent stats, we are becoming more connected technologically, but less so socially.

As with any cultural transformation in history, the rise of postmodernism brought astonishing change in many different ways. Technological advances has affected our culture in more ways than we sometimes

---

[5] Ibid.

admit. One article says that:

> Young people's attachment to their mobile phones is eroding their personal relationships, according to a new study. The claims come after research revealed that young adults - in addition to sending over 100 texts - check their mobile up to 60 times a day. Experts behind a new study have now said compulsively checking a mobile phone is an addiction similar to compulsive spending or credit card misuse.[6]

It goes on:

> Dr. James Roberts, of the Baylor's Hankamer School of Business, said it was important for students who spend up to seven hours a day interacting with communication technology to recognise when their behaviour is becoming a problem. 'Mobile phones are a part of our consumer culture,' Dr. Roberts said. 'They are not just a consumer tool, but are used as a status symbol. 'They're also eroding our personal relationships,' he added... Dr. Roberts and his team said that, for the majority of young people, losing their phone would be 'disastrous to their social lives'.[7]

What is certain is that we are bringing much of this

---

[6] "It's probably better to talk: How checking our phones 60 times a day is driving away friends," *Mail Online* (December 1, 2012), http://www.dailymail.co.uk/news/article-2241326/It-s-probably-better-talk-How-checking-phones-60-times-day-driving-away-friends.html.

[7] Ibid.

problem of loneliness on ourselves. Facebook, Twitter, technology, etc., is something that is morally neutral and yet we can use these things either for the glory of God for the glory of ourselves. When we glorify ourselves, we are glorying in self-righteousness, and that is wickedness.

What I do not want to do is belittle those who feel lonely, so please do not get that from what I just said. Some of our loneliness is not our fault. Several people have been abandoned, left alone, and circumstances do play a role; but I think if we are honest, many of us have brought it upon ourselves as the previous two articles have articulated.

So what is the answer to loneliness? How do we deal with loneliness in our society? How do we, as Christians, deal with the glories of the gospel and fight for joy while fighting against this issue of loneliness—especially if we've been created for community? If our calling is community, where do we go from here? It is time to turn to the text.

GOSPEL PARTNERSHIP

The fight for joy while alone opens up Paul's letter to the Philippians. It is here where the centrality of the gospel meets Paul where he's at: *prison*. He is alone, with no friends nearby to help him. Proximity is not going to help him—not when you are isolated in a Roman jail cell hundreds of miles away. Affinity is not the answer—his core team is remarkably different. What can help?

When sentenced to prison in ancient times, one was condemned to loneliness. You were not given food or a phone call, and you certainly did not have the assurance of ever getting out. Paul is acutely aware of the fact that this may not end well for him (1:21). He is exhausted from his travels, too. What might Paul say, then, given this circumstance?

Keep in mind that the context of this next section is "grace" and "peace." Paul is always talking about grace—unmerited favor in Jesus—and peace, the result of said grace. Paul is gospel-centered, meaning that everything comes back to the gospel and its importance both for identity, and for the mission of making disciples.

Paul begins in verse 3 by thanking God in his remembrance of the Philippian people. Who could blame Paul for this prayer of remembrance? In the previous chapter, I laid out the story of the Philippian church. They are a motley-crew-of-a-church-planting-group that consisted of a rich woman (Lydia) a formerly demon-possessed slave girl, and a Roman jailer. Oh what stories Paul must have remembered! For whatever reason, Paul is joyful, and he expresses this joy with *thanksgiving*.

Herein lies yet another way to fight for joy: being thankful for everything. The blessings we enjoy now pale in comparison to eternity. Paul, who is alone, gives thanks. He remembers the Philippian Christians, and it brings him deep and abiding joy.

Paul connects this thanksgiving with prayer in the next verse (4). In "every prayer" he is thankful, and it brings him joy. In other words, whenever Paul prays for them, he is always thankful for them. When the Spirit brings to Paul's mind the Philippian church, he joyfully prays for them with thanksgiving. Fee expounds:

> Joy, it should be noted, which occurs only here in the Pauline thanksgivings, lies at the heart of the Christian experience of the gospel; it is the fruit of the Spirit in any truly Christian life, serving as primary evidence of the Spirit's presence (Gal 5:22; Rom 14:17). Precisely because this is so, joy transcends the present circumstances; it is based altogether on the Spirit, God's way of being present with his people under the new covenant. Hence joy prevails for Paul even in prison; he will urge that it prevail for the Philippians as well in their present suffering in the face of opposition.[8]

The Apostle Paul knows quite intimately the role of the Spirit in his life. He understands that joy is a fruit (Gal. 5:22). He also recognizes that in order to endure much pain and suffering, he must rely on the Spirit to grant him this gift. Furthermore, the Spirit's work in the life of a believer is gospel-centered. As the Holy Spirit works in the life of the Christian, he draws him near to cross. He (the Spirit) desires to glorify Jesus so that the Father is glorified, and the believer is satisfied. The Trinity is at work in all of life.

Moreover, Paul situates this prayer of thanksgiving with joy within the context of the "partnership in the gospel" that he has with his beloved friends (1:5). The

---

[8] Gordon D. Fee, *Paul's Letter to the Philippians* (Grand Rapids, MI: W.B Eerdmans Pub. Co., 1995), 81.

word "partnership" in Greek is *koinonia* and denotes the idea of sharing in something. (Paul uses the word six times in this letter). It is sometimes translated as "fellowship," or "participation." Fellowship often evokes images of church potluck dinners and zero conversation about Jesus. So we must be careful using this word. The idea is that two or more people have entered into a common association.

"Partnership" is a solid translation because it conveys the idea of not only this common goal, but of a joyful joining together of parties who might not normally do something together. For Paul, he is joined together with the church and united under the commonality of the gospel message. He is thankful (with joy!) that they have joined hands with him in the cause of the spread of the gospel.

The gospel is everything to Paul (I will expand on the various elements of Paul's view of the gospel throughout the book). When I say "gospel," I do not mean mere information about the Christ event.[9] I mean Paul's actual encounter with the living Christ and his relationship with him *now*. Paul is less concerned about gospel as mere proclamation, and more concerned about Jesus himself.[10]

---

[9] "Christ event" is shorthand for Jesus' preexistence, incarnation, life, death, burial, resurrection, ascension, and subsequent intercession right now. At the center is his atoning work on the cross and subsequent vindication in resurrection.

[10] See Gordon D. Fee, *Paul's Letter to the Philippians* (Grand Rapids, MI: W.B Eerdmans Pub. Co., 1995), 82.

This partnership is an intimate experience based upon Paul and the Philippians' abiding connection with the Lord. They do not have much else in common, which is further evidence that proximity and affinity are not the answer to loneliness. The thing that unites them is not a thing, but a person—the Lord, Jesus Christ.

I think that the true answer to loneliness lies in gospel partnership. How else can two entirely opposite people with differing delights, hobbies and emotions ever unite? How else can someone who enjoys sports ever become close with someone who unreservedly despises sports? Setting the extremes aside for a moment, I wish to make known that Jesus is everything. If Jesus is not everything, than he is nothing—there is no such thing as lukewarm Christianity. There's only Jesus Christianity. And Jesus unites the most diverse of people through the gospel.

Think about this for a moment as it pertains to the local church. You (I assume?) and I are part of a local body. We are, for the sake of argument, joined into something outside of ourselves. It does not matter if you are reading this as a parishioner of the church I pastor, or someone from another country in another local church: the reality is, you and I are *adopted*. God is our Father, and Jesus is our older brother. We are a *family*. This is the basis of gospel partnership. The world may be found alone, but Christians, especially, ought *never* to be found alone! We are sons and daughters, brothers and sisters of our heavenly Father. And oh how he loves! God is a *good* Father who loves to take care of his children. Loneliness is defeated when we grasp this truth about

God.

Paul is enthusiastic that the Philippians *understand* the gospel and have chosen to *participate* in the gospel through their gift of sustenance. He is savoring the fact that they do not simply *know about* it—they *live it*. The local church is God's primary means of gospel partnership. Are you in one? Not only are you in one, are you an active part of one? Are you a part of a gospel community on mission? This brings immense joy to our Father in heaven; to see his children living as missional servants bringing himself glory.

GOD IS NOT FINISHED WITH YOU

One of the greatest verses in the scripture is Philippians 1:6 which says, "And I am sure of this, that he who began a good work in you will bring it to completion at the day of Jesus Christ." Paul does not say that God might consider bringing it to completion if we are good; he does not say that God is incapable of brining us to completion. No, he says that he *will*. What a glorious truth is the doctrine of perseverance of the saints.

This verse promises that what God has started, he will finish. Not only is this true on the larger scale of creation and redemption of all things (Rom. 8), but it is also true in your heart. When the Holy Spirit regenerates the heart and faith is gifted, and a person responds with repentance, he is a Christian. This is the "good work" that Paul is talking about, and good it is. From here a person has begun the arduous process of growing in holiness (a holiness that derives from Jesus); and Paul reminds us that self-improvement or self-reliance is not the answer. The pursuit of holiness is a pursuit of Jesus who is our holiness. God does not begin a good work in someone only to leave them to their own moral efforts to improve themselves. No, God "will bring it to completion." It is God who works in the believer as Paul will rationalize later (2:12).[11]

Perseverance of the Saints says that God the Holy Spirit is the *preserver* of us, and he alone works to keep us on track for redemption. Those who have genuine faith will endure to the end because God will keep them; those who do not persevere never had genuine faith. R.C. Sproul is helpful here:

> I think this little catchphrase, *perseverance of the saints*, is dangerously misleading. It suggests that the perseverance is something that we do, perhaps in and of ourselves. I believe that saints do persevere in faith, and that those who have been effectually called by God and have been reborn by the power of the Holy Spirit endure to the end. However, they persevere not because they are so diligent in making use of the mercies of God. The only reason we can give why any of us continue on in the faith is because we have been preserved. So I prefer the term *the preservation of the saints*, because the process by which we are kept in a state of grace is something that is accomplished by God. My confidence in my preservation is not in my ability

---

[11] "In other words, those who will be saved in the future live holy lives in the present, but the holiness that characterizes their lives is God's work from beginning to end." Frank Thielman, *Philippians*, The NIV Application Commentary (Grand Rapids, MI: Zondervan Publishing House, 1995). 39.

to persevere. My confidence rests in the power of
Christ to sustain me with His grace and by the power of
His intercession. He is going to bring us safely home.[12]

Part of the beauty of the glorious doctrines of grace is
that it all goes back to God and his doing, his glory, and
his grace. May our boasting be mortified.

So here is Paul, grateful for the Philippian church and
their partnership in the furtherance of the gospel. Paul
is alone, and they send him a gift (4:15). He is thankful
for them. But he is still alone. And this loneliness does
not stop him. He has partnered and unified them as a
family under the common Lordship of Jesus. Not only
this, Paul knows that what Jesus has started, he will
finish. Paul knows that God is not done with his life, and
loneliness not absolute. He understands that God is a
finisher and that sin will not win. These are powerful
tools that Paul has given us to combat loneliness. How
will you use them?

Paul's discourse has only just begun, however. He
writes, "It is right for me to feel this way about you all,
because I hold you in my heart" (1:7a). He clings to their
partnership in the gospel, knowing that they are
cherished in his heart. Not only does he remember
them, but he loves them, deeply.

The reason for this recollection is because they are

---

[12] R.C. Sproul, "TULIP and Reformed Theology: Perseverance of the
Saints." *Ligonier Ministries* (blog), December 5, 2012,
http://www.ligonier.org/blog/tulip-and-reformed-theology-
perseverance-saints/.

"all partakers with [Paul] of grace, both in [his] imprisonment and in the defense and confirmation of the gospel" (1:7b). Paul, in his loneliness in prison, fights for joy, and has an everlasting partnership in the gospel with the Philippians who have joined him in the "defense and confirmation" of the gospel message. These are legal terms closely related to the doctrine of justification that Paul will hint at in verse 11 and elsewhere throughout the book. As Paul suffers, he knows that he has enjoined himself to his beloved church. They are defending and confirming that the gospel can and will go forward, regardless of circumstances.

Even if things do not go well, Paul says, "For God is my witness, how I yearn for you all with the affection of Christ Jesus" (1:8). This is a strong gospel partnership, one that is based upon "grace" (1:7a). He understands that the gospel *vindicates*. And even if he dies alone, he will not really die alone; and neither will the Philippian church. Both parties have a profound connection to the grace of Christ. This grace is predominant in gospel participation.

If you are lonely, please understand that God is not finished with you. He is actively working out all things for your good (Rom. 8:28). Loneliness is temporary, but eternity with Christ is forever. Paul's mindset in these few verses is rooted in gospel partnership and this keeps him going through the power of the Holy Spirit.

PURE AND BLAMELESS
The apostle is going to finish out this section and help us

deal with the issue of loneliness as it pertains to the doctrine of justification.

> And it is my prayer that your love may abound more and more, with knowledge and all discernment, so that you may approve what is excellent, and so be pure and blameless for the day of Christ, filled with the fruit of righteousness that comes through Jesus Christ, to the glory and praise of God.[13]

What is certain about loneliness is that it is a struggle to believe. It is a struggle to believe that we have value, dignity and worth. It is a struggle to believe what it our identity *is* now that we've been justified by faith. Piper writes:

> The gospel of Christ crucified and risen is meant to be preached to the soul—both in corporate worship where we hear it week after week, and from hour to hour as we preach it to ourselves in the daily fight for joy. The message of the cross has a central and unique place in the fight for joy.[14]

Piper is unquestionably correct: the gospel is central, and the identity we receive from it is where joy is to be fought. This is a daily fight to preach "to the soul."

Paul begins this prayer report with the *what*: That the

---

[13] Phil. 1:9-11.

[14] John Piper, *When I Don't Desire God: How to Fight for Joy* (Wheaton, IL: Crossway Books, 2004), 76.

Philippians' (1) love may abound more and more; which results in (2) knowledge and discernment; so that they can (3) approve what is excellent, (4) and be filled with the fruit of righteousness. *Why* all of this happens is so that they may be pure and blameless. *How* this happens is from Jesus Christ, and the *goal* is for the glory and praise of God. This is how Paul helps the church understand loneliness and understand how they are to fight for joy.

To fight for joy in loneliness is to fight for love. The love that Paul foresees is a love for one another in gospel partnership. "Whoever says he is in the light and hates his brother is still in darkness" (1 Jn. 2:9). Brotherly and sisterly affection and love require us to see the other person as valuable, precious, and worth more than our own lives. "Greater love has no one than this, that someone lay down his life for his friends" (Jn. 15:13).

And this is precisely what Jesus has done. He has laid down his own life for his friends. If we are to fight for joy while alone, we must be able to stare at the cross and remember where our identity stands. Because of this, Paul will return to Jesus in just two more verses.

Paul's desire is for the Philippian church to see love abound more and more, *with knowledge and discernment.* To elaborate:

> Paul's basic request for the Philippians, in other words, is that they might express their love in ways that show both a knowledge of how to obey God's will generally, and, more specifically, of how to make moral decisions

based on God's will in the give-and-take of everyday living.[15]

Paul wishes for the church to not only love, but love according to the will of God, and live with wisdom. At the heart of it is a desire for the Philippian church to "approve what is excellent" (1:10a). The hope is that, as the battle for the fight for joy rages on, the church will not waver doctrinally from the fruit of righteousness that comes from Jesus.

Herein lies the heart of the truth of the gospel that Paul sets forth. He says that this fruit of righteousness "comes through Jesus Christ" (vs. 11). The context of Paul's logic is fixed on "the day of Jesus Christ" in 1:6. This eschatological framework is something that Paul keeps in mind often in the fight for joy. Fee writes:

> What Paul wants is for them to stand on *that* day "*full* of the fruit of righteousness." But to do so they must *now* be *living out* such righteousness.[16]

In other words, the fight for joy while alone is a fight to: (1) Remember where you have been (or to be more specific, remember what Christ *did*) and (2) remember where you are going. In order to battle loneliness through partnership in the gospel, we must be "pure

---

[15] Frank Thielman, *Philippians*, The NIV Application Commentary (Grand Rapids, MI: Zondervan Publishing House, 1995). 41.

[16] Gordon D. Fee, *Paul's Letter to the Philippians* (Grand Rapids, MI: W.B Eerdmans Pub. Co., 1995), 103.

and blameless."

How can we be pure and blameless when God is holy, and we are sinful? The answer? *Justification by faith.*

Justification is the doctrine that says that you and I, though sinful, can stand in front of God the Judge and be avowed, "Not guilty," based upon the person and work of Jesus Christ. We could never stand on our own; our works are atrocious to God (Is. 64:6). But since we are declared not guilty because of Jesus, we do not have to pay the penalty incurred by our sin, for Jesus did that for us at the cross.

However, this doctrine does not stop there. We are given Christ's righteousness (2 Cor. 5:21), and when God looks at us, it is as though we'd never sinned, *and* as though we'd always obeyed. Paul finishes this section by saying that our calling is to be pure and blameless. The basis for this occurrence can only happen because of Jesus and what he has done in justifying us. We work from our justification, not for it. And this for the glory and praise of God.

The fight for joy is a fight to see, and the fight to see is a fight to savor Christ, and the fight to savor Christ results in joy. Loneliness is defeated when you realize what Christ has done for you. When you realize that he has declared you righteous—acquitting you of your sin no less—you can rejoice with your gospel partners, welcomed together in the glorious grace found at the foot of the cross. When you understand the gospel and your identity that is wrapped up inside of it, you are able to rejoice at what God has done, and celebrate this *together* as partners in the good news.

Paul is alone, imprisoned for his faith. Nevertheless, he fights for joy while alone by seeing and savoring Jesus Christ and remembering his friends. Though they are far from him, he can delight in this partnership that sees the gospel go forward, even amidst suffering.

3 - WHEN SUFFERING

*I want you to know, brothers, that what has happened to me
has really served to advance the gospel, so that it has become
known throughout the whole imperial guard and to all the
rest that my imprisonment is for Christ. And most of the
brothers, having become confident in the Lord by my
imprisonment, are much more bold to speak the word without
fear. Some indeed preach Christ from envy and rivalry, but
others from good will. The latter do it out of love, knowing
that I am put here for the defense of the gospel. The former
proclaim Christ out of selfish ambition, not sincerely but
thinking to afflict me in my imprisonment. What then? Only
that in every way, whether in pretense or in truth, Christ is
proclaimed, and in that I rejoice.*[1]

This chapter is an incredibly difficult one to write
because as a pastor, I have found that joy and
suffering are intimately connected. I do not have

---

[1] Phil. 1:12-18.

the luxury of officiating baby dedications and weddings exclusively. I must also do funerals. During the "in-between" of life as we wait for our final glorification, joy and suffering will be two sides of the same coin for everyone. In the gospel, we *have been* saved from the *penalty* of sin, we *are being saved* from the *power* of sin, and we *will be saved* from the *presence* of sin. We are a work in progress. This gospel is crucial to understand when dealing with every issue you and I will face, but it is especially key in the fight for joy when suffering.

In 2012, I had been a part of various suffering, not just myself, but with many in my congregation. From child to adult, I've seen cancer take lives, divorces run rampant, families battle sickness all of the time, finances fall apart for people, job loss, depression, anxiety, stress, loneliness, and friendships end at the drop of a hat. As I write this, we are approaching Christmas 2012, and just yesterday I received news of a woman who is losing her battle with cancer and has only a few months left to live. On top of this, a gentleman in our church is also battling a brain malfunction that has caused strokes and other issues. Even still, as I go back to edit this chapter, there was another school shooting, this time at Sandy Hook Elementary School in Newtown, CT. Most days I find myself begging God to come. Now.

This issue of suffering is a tricky subject to tackle. For me, it brings back memories of the summer of 1994 when my mother battled (and defeated) leukemia. This was incredibly formative for me at the young age of twelve.[2] Not only that, it is difficult to deal with this issue because it affects each of us. No one is exempt from suffering. At some point in your life, you will suffer. We are either on the giving end of suffering (e.g., the suffering we caused our mothers when we were born), or the receiving end of suffering. Suffering is inescapable.

Furthermore, the subject is tricky because we tend to make several errors when processing suffering. More on this later.

Please understand that suffering should never be taken lightly. Oftentimes we play the comparative game when discussing suffering. If someone has suffered something that was exceptionally traumatizing for them, we ought not to condescendingly belittle their suffering in an attempt to demonstrate how our suffering was far worse. Put yourself in their shoes for a moment and remember that suffering can be anything from a paper cut, to a broken leg; from a car accident to cancer. All of this is suffering. And all of it is meaningful to each of us in a unique way. It is better to empathize than denigrate.

To offer even further clarification on where I'm coming from, I'll define suffering as the affliction of the head, heart and hands. It is pain, both emotional and physical. It could be uncomfortable emotions and negative feelings that are a result of sinful influence. It could be persistent back pain. It could be the stress of an

---

[2] My "call" to pastoral ministry is intimately connected to this experience of suffering.

impossible situation at work. Whatever the concern, it is anything that is contrary to the glory of God. In other words, it is a result of sin in a fallen, broken, and rebellious creation. Whether it is a tornado, or the feeling you get when someone calls you a name—suffering is a part of this world, but will not be a part of the world to come.

What I hope to accomplish in this chapter is *not* somehow to give all the right answers and copiously rationalize why God allows suffering. To do so would be unhelpful because my extrapolations would dare to venture inside the mind of God and no man has done this. Furthermore, I do not wish to answer all of the questions that are out there, nor do I wish to try to get behind the philosophy of it all. What I intend to do is provoke thought and get behind the mind of Paul in this section of Philippians. I want to see how it is he fought for joy when suffering.

BIBLICAL EXAMPLES OF SUFFERING

There are lot's of examples of suffering in the Bible. From the very first murder (Cain killing Abel) to the final judgment and eternal sentencing to hell of those who have rejected Christ, you can find suffering on just about every page of the Bible. For example, in the Old Testament the story of Joseph provides the perfect illustration.

Joseph was the second youngest son of the patriarch Jacob. Jacob favored Joseph over the other brothers and because of it he spoiled him tremendously. Remember that he even gave him the infamous coat with many different colors.

Things took a turn for the worst when Joseph told his brothers about the dreams he was having. In his dreams, his brothers bowed down to him. They didn't like this, so they conspired against him, selling him as a slave and reporting to their father that he was dead.

As years passed, Joseph rose to the top of Pharaoh's advisory board, being the right-hand-man for all things political. After a string of events, Joseph ended up in prison, and then released on account of his skill at dream interpretation. He warned the Pharaoh of a coming famine and was able to help the nation prepare for the devastation.

As the story goes on, Jacob sends his sons to Egypt for help because of the famine. The sons who had originally sold Joseph into slavery eventually show up in front of their brother's throne. Joseph recognized them, but the brothers were slow to notice Joseph. Eventually it is discovered, and the feelings of remorse set in for the brothers who betrayed Joseph. They apologized to him, and Joseph responds with one of the most profound statements in all of Scripture:

> As for you, you meant evil against me, but God meant it for good, to bring about that many people should be kept alive, as they are today.[3]

Joseph's brothers, in their sinful envy committed evil

---

[3] Genesis 50:20.

against him. But their act of evil was never the final answer before the Throne of Divine Sovereignty. What the Bible makes abundantly clear is that no matter what the evil intent, no matter what plan is devised by the likes of sinful man, God, in his divine providence uses all means to achieve his ends.

> God's works of providence are, His most holy, wise, and powerful preserving and governing of his creatures, and all their actions.[4]

In accordance to his own free will, God keeps all things in place, is involved in all events and governs all of this to their suitable end. He rules all things and orchestrates all things to accomplish his purposes. God is big. And majestic. And providential.

> The Bible clearly teaches God's providential control (1) over the universe at large, Ps. 103:19; Dan. 4:35; Eph. 1:11; (2) over the physical world, Job 37; Ps. 104:14; 135:6; Mt. 5:45; (3) over the brute creation, Ps. 104:21, 28; Mt. 6:26; 10:29; (4) over the affairs of nations, Job 12:23; Ps. 22:28; 66:7; Acts 17:26; (5) over man's birth and lot in life, 1 Sam. 16:1; Ps. 139:16; Is. 45:5; Gal. 1:15, 16; (6) over the outward successes and failures of men's lives, Ps. 75:6, 7; Lk.1:52; (7) over things seemingly accidental or insignificant, Pr. 16:33; Mt. 10:30; (8) in the protection of the righteous, Ps. 4:8; 5:12; 63:8; 121:3; Rom. 8:28; (9) in supplying the wants of God's people,

---

[4] Question 11, *The Westminster Shorter Catechism: With Scripture Proofs*, 3rd edition. (Oak Harbor, WA: Logos Research Systems, Inc., 1996).

Gn. 22:8; 14; Dt. 8:3; Phil. 4:19; (10) in giving answers to prayer, 1 Sam. 1:19; Is. 20:5, 6; 2 Chr. 33:13; Ps. 65:2; Mt. 7:7; Lk. 18:7, 8; and (11) in the exposure and punishment of the wicked, Ps. 7:12, 13; 11:6.[5]

If we are to deal with the problem of suffering head on, we must be as biblical as possible. We must sit on *sola scriptura* and remember that the Bible is authoritative. So many people (Christians nonetheless!) try to explain their position on anything without the use of Scripture, but instead try to construct an argument based on something else, be it philosophy or experience or tradition. When we deal with suffering, there is nothing sturdier to stand on than God's inerrant and infallible word. We need the objective truth of Scripture to inform our minds.

There is yet another profound example of suffering in the Bible.

The story of Job is a masterful piece of literature. Situated in the Old Testament, Job is the story of a righteous man named Job who is brought under the grip of suffering. Satan and God have a conversation about this man and God grants Satan the ability to crush Job— but not kill him—and do so by any means necessary. (Satan thinks that Job will curse God, but God does believe he will).

Satan proceeds to rip Job's life apart by taking his family and possessions and even his health (2:1-10).

---

[5] Louis Berkhof, *Systematic Theology* 2d rev. ed. (Grand Rapids: MI: Wm. B. Eerdmans Publishing Co., 1941), 168.

Throughout all of this suffering, Job does not murmur a word of sin or blasphemy against God (2:10).

The bulk of the book is a poetic discourse revolving around Job and his unhelpful friends. They accuse him of sin and an unrepentant heart, but Job is resolute in his blamelessness. He has some serious questions for God. The biggest mistake his friends make is believing that there is a spiritual problem with Job. They believe that Job must have sinned and done something wrong, otherwise he would not have to endure such suffering. Countless people fall into this trap of over-spiritualization.

At the end of the story, God asks Job the "Where were you?" question (38:4). It humbles and brings clarity to Job, and the book closes by God blessing Job beyond what he had ever had beforehand.

I am aware that this is probably an oversimplification, and I have not done comprehensive justice to the story. It is a long book with many complex issues, but I wanted you to get the gist of it. Job is about suffering, and the theory of moralization is shown to be impotent by this book.

The last biblical example of suffering that I wish to examine is appropriately held for last because the subject is our Lord. If anyone suffered most, it was Jesus, the Son of God.

Jesus' life as the Man of Sorrows is full of joy and trial. From the very beginning of his life, his parents had to flee for fear of King Herod coming to kill their newborn baby (Mt. 2:1-18). Throughout his ministry, he faced lot's of suffering:

1. Temptation by Satan (Mk. 1:12-13)

2. Accusations of blasphemy (Mk. 2:7), law breaking (Mk. 2:24), insanity (Mk. 3:21), demon-possession (Mk. 3:22), tradition/rule breaking (Mk. 7:5), and plenty of other things.

3. He was nearly killed early on in his ministry (Lk. 4:29).

4. He was illegally tried, beaten and murdered.

Jesus was truly the Man of Sorrows, heavily acquainted with grief. If ever anyone has suffered, it was this man who was tempted in every way like us but never sinned (Heb. 4:15). His suffering is beyond our comprehension as Western Christians. Just watch *The Passion of the Christ* and you will quickly learn how gruesome his suffering truly was. The beating he took, coupled with the immense pain of suffocation in crucifixion, was horrible. Jesus is *the* Sufferer.

Moreover, there are plenty of other examples outside of the Scriptures. For instance, we know from church history and the writings of the early Christians that Paul was beheaded, and Peter crucified upside down. Many Christians throughout the centuries were killed for their belief. William Tyndale was burned at the stake for translating the Bible into the English language. What was it that helped them through their suffering? While there are no easy answers, there are some answers, and we will get there shortly.

ERRORS IN ASSESSING SUFFERING

At the start of this chapter, I mentioned a couple of brief things that we tend to do when coping with the problem of suffering. One of the obvious things that we do sometimes is blame God. To clarify, God is not the author of evil, though he does allow it, works to redeem it, and uses it to achieve his purposes (we saw this in the story of Joseph). Many times we ask God, "Where were you?"; or even "Why didn't you intervene?" I have frequently asked God for a sign to help me make a decision. When I do not see a clear sign from him, I blame him for making the wrong one when it was my own knuckle-headedness that caused the problem. This is not helpful. Criticizing God for our failure is simply blame-shifting and does nothing to prove our finite case.

Another thing we get caught doing is like Job's friends, we over-spiritualize suffering. Our love for retribution theology quickly kicks in when we see someone suffering. For example, a friend of mine whom I was supervising at the time was battling sickness for about a month or two. It was one of those situations where everything was going wrong, and nothing seemed to go right. He broke his wrist, had the flu, followed that up with a cold, contracted the flu *again* and then his family all became sick. On top of this, his car stopped working and needed considerable repair, and he even received two paper cuts in the same spot on the same day. Okay, so I'm exaggerating the last part about the paper cuts, but the rest is true. The man was seriously out of control! Nothing was going right for him.

Have you ever said, "When it rains, it pours"? He did.

Not only that, he asked me if there was sin in his life that he had not repented of. While I could not tell if he was saying this in jest or not, I think deep down he truly wondered. We had a brief discussion about it, and I told him I do not think God works this way, though Paul says in 1 Corinthians 11:29-30 that some have misused the Lord's Supper and consequently drank "judgment" on themselves. He goes on to say that this "is why many of you are weak and ill, and some have died." This is a descriptive passage, rather than prescriptive, however, the mystery is still there and far beyond the scope of this book.

At any rate, my friend over-spiritualized it by claiming that God is somehow seeking vengeance on him. For the Christian, we know that our Father does and will discipline us, but not out of wrath, it is out of love (Heb. 12:6). We can safely rule out the misinformed idea that God is "getting you back" through revenge by making you suffer.

A few years ago, I was doing youth ministry in Philadelphia. On one particular evening, the car that belonged to a colleague of mine had broken down. She arrived late to our youth gathering and professed that Satan had attacked her car, thus preventing her to come in a timely manner. Aside from a poor theology of Satan, I was flabbergasted by this statement. *I seriously do not believe that Satan is all that worried about your car*, I thought.[6]

---

[6] Let me say at this point that there are two types of Christians in this arena of belief: 1) Either you take Satan way too seriously, and give

In his book *Glorious Ruin*, Tullian Tchividjian spells out two extremes when dealing with suffering. He calls them "moralizing" and "minimizing." Regarding this issue of over-spiritualization (moralizing), he writes:

> Christians believe that Jesus severed the link between suffering and deserving once for all on Calvary. God put the ledgers away and settled the accounts. But when you and I insist on that all-too-comfortable paradigm of cosmic score keeping, we stop talking about Christianity and in fact adopt a Westernized form of Hinduism. We are talking about karma. If you are a bad person and things are going well for you, it is only a matter of time before karma catches up with you and "you get yours." If you are a good, the inverse is true: just be patient and your good deeds will come back to you.[7]

He is right. One of the biggest threats to our dealing with suffering is the temptation to bring in a debauched theology that says our performance is how we earn and keep God's favor. When we have a view of God that is akin to Santa Claus, we will not be able to deal with suffering in biblical terms, but instead will adopt a

---

him powers that he does not possess (like reading your mind); or 2) You do not take him seriously enough and ignore the fact that there is a large war happening in the spiritual realm (Eph. 5:12). Do not, however, make the mistake of thinking that Satan is omniscient and omnipresent.

[7] Tullian Tchividjian, *Glorious Ruin* (Colorado Springs, CO: David C Cook, 2012), 100.

response spotlighted on karma. Instead of resting on biblical truth, we will rest on our presumptions. Instead of aligning our thoughts with God's word, we choose to believe something contrary about him. The gospel says that God's love is lavished upon us in Christ even when we do not obey, and seemingly cannot obey. If we are to deal with suffering accurately, we cannot be so focused on ourselves that we blame shift, or over-spiritualize it. We must rest in the grace of God found in Christ and our subsequent identity therein. The way we deal with suffering is focusing more on Christ and less on our ever-changing circumstances. Over-spiritualization under values God and his outrageous grace.

The other significant error we propagate when dealing with suffering is when we trivialize (or as Tchividjian says, "minimize") it.

> Minimization involves any attempt to downplay or reduce the extent and nature of pain. Any rhetorical or spiritual device that underestimates the seriousness of suffering essentially minimizes it. Quick fixes are inevitably minimizing tactics. Platitudes are minimizing tactics. If moralization reduces suffering to a moral or spiritual issue, minimization makes similar reductions.[8]

What's at stake here is not only a false humility ("It's no big deal, people do this all of the time"), but a complete denial of how God works in and through suffering ("It

---

[8] Ibid., 120.

will be okay, God does not want his children to suffer").
Here's what I mean.

Have you ever said, for example, "Wow, I'm sorry
that you're feeling a certain way. It will get better." Or
maybe you have found yourself telling someone who is
suffering, "You're going to get through this, just keep
thinking positively."

These are all illustrations of "quick fixes" and
"platitudes". Instead of tackling the issue of suffering
head-on, we trivialize it by explaining it away and
minimizing it as something that is of no concern. If we
are to deal with suffering, we cannot do this; we have to
call a spade a "spade" and go from there. To explain
these things away by making them feel like less of an
issue, we adopt the "out of sight, out of mind" attitude
and never experience the grace of God found in
suffering. We'd rather help ourselves and use our own
moral effort to manage our suffering (and sin, for that
matter).

TWO THEOLOGIES TO THINK THROUGH

The celebrated Reformer Martin Luther, wrote about
two different theologies that we must think through
when dealing with the issue of suffering. (These
theologies work in all facets of life, not just suffering,
but for this chapter it will be the focus).

The first is called the "theology of glory." In this
theology, God is seen only through victory. It is the most
natural inclination of the self-righteous human heart
plagued with sin. Suffering is just a result of sin (true),
but in this theology, it is a mere setback towards a

bigger and brighter future. Think about the stereotypical television preacher. That should give you an idea of what this theology says. This theology believes that suffering is some small concern that can only lead to some greater end. Getting back on the road to glory is the only concern for this person. If we can simply improve our thoughts and have a better attitude, we can get rid of this suffering and move forward. This person uses the Holy Spirit as a mere coping mechanism—a crutch and a step on the way to feeling better. If we trivialize or over-spiritualize suffering, we can reconstruct a better future and suffering will somehow hurt less. We will not have to feel the pain because physical pain is evil, and spiritual bliss is good.[9]

The far superior approach to theology is the "theology of the cross." Luther believed that the cross is our only theology (*crux sola est nostra theologia*). In this theology, God is seen through defeat, weakness, vulnerability, and *suffering*. It is a supernatural work of God in the hearts of wicked men to be able to perceive this as Paul lays out so clearly in 1 Corinthians 1:18-25.[10] Instead of seeing God as distant and only there for us in the good times, the theology of the cross says that there are no truly good (joy) times apart from the work of Christ, and the work of Christ is centered on the

---

[9] This is a sweeping theological problem known as platonic dualism. *Google* it sometime when you have a moment. It shows its ugly head in the gnostic tendencies of some "Christian" theology.

[10] "For the word of the cross is folly to those who are perishing, but to us who are being saved it is the power of God" (1 Cor. 1:18).

scandalous cross. The reason there are no true good things apart from him is because anything but the infinite value and worth of Christ is just an over-promising, under-delivering, idol. We are not to "move on to bigger and better things" because there is nothing bigger and better than God. When suffering, we fight for joy, not by trivializing or over-spiritualizing suffering; we confess that God is present in it and that he is our joy ready and willing to weep with us. The theologian of the cross sees suffering as real, calls it for what it is, and believes by faith that God is using it for his good (Rom. 8:28). What is crucial to remember is that suffering is very much a part of this fallen world and that God is not shocked by it. Instead, God enters into it in order to make his glory known and show himself sufficient and all-satisfying as well as supreme, just, gracious and powerful. The Man of Sorrows did not drive around in his fancy car spitting out presumptuous platitudes. No, he came and died so that we could have life. Our job is to run out of fresh fabrications of false hope so that our only hope will be our Only Hope.

As Christians, we do not go the *reductio ad absurdum* route, somehow reducing suffering down to an easy explanation with all of the right answers. Rather, we grow near to God knowing that he is growing near to us.

Suffering is best dealt with by realizing that God is actively a part of it *with you*. He is not distantly looking for you to pick yourself up by your own moral bootstraps. He is close to you, wooing you back to the cross to remember that he loves you and that no matter the outcome, he is using it for his glory and our good.

That is the key to fighting for joy when suffering.

THE TEXT

Having laid the foundation for suffering and how we should respond to it, I want to take us back to the text here in Philippians. Paul has just opened up his letter, and you can envisage the anguish his beloved brothers and sisters must be feeling as they read this letter aloud. Keep in mind that Epaphroditus is to deliver this letter to them and no doubt they are worried about Paul. They know something has gone awry because they know he is in jail. They are also anxiously awaiting to find out what exactly has happened to him. Instead of telling them about himself, however, he talks about the gospel. Paul is deeply gospel-centered, and this is what he says right from the start:

> I want you to know, brothers, that what has happened to me has really served to advance the gospel, so that it has become known throughout the whole imperial guard and to all the rest that my imprisonment is for Christ. And most of the brothers, having become confident in the Lord by my imprisonment, are much more bold to speak the word without fear.[11]

"What has happened" to Paul is imprisonment; but not only imprisonment, *suffering*, as well. Paul has had a rough go as an evangelist/church planter. (A cursory reading of 2 Corinthians will give you glimpse into his

---

[11] Phil. 1:12-14.

suffering). He reports back to the Philippian church that, though it looks disadvantageous in terms of human worldview, what has happened to him has actually turned out to be good because the gospel is going forward.

For Paul, he understands the theology of the cross. He knows that the greatest act of suffering led to vindication. Jesus' suffering was horrendous, yet God vindicated him by resurrecting him. Paul gets that afflictions and troubles are going to come, and he understands that Jesus did it for him. If God can use Jesus' suffering for redemptive purposes, then God will use his suffering for redemptive purposes, too. This is where Paul goes in verse 13 by saying that his imprisonment is "for Christ" (literally, "in Christ").

The reason Paul can view it this way is because of the objective truth of the cross, and the fact that this suffering has served as an opportunity to advance the gospel message. Instead of sulking in the emotions of anxiety and frustration, he embraces whatever circumstance comes his way as an opportunity to tell people about Jesus.

How do you fight for joy, Paul?

"By knowing that I am "in Christ," and being in Christ means not only that Jesus suffered for me, and not only that I am in prison for the sake of Christ, but that I am actively participating in Christ's afflictions, too."[12]

---

[12] "Now I rejoice in my sufferings for your sake, and in my flesh I am filling up what is lacking in Christ's afflictions for the sake of his body, that is, the church" (Col. 1:24).

> Thus [Paul's] imprisonment is not simply a result of his Christian commitment but is the necessary means through which Paul fulfills his calling. It is not only "for Christ" but "in Christ" as well.[13]

If you recall, when Jesus saved Paul on the road to Damascus, Paul was the cause of much suffering for followers of Jesus. Curiously, Jesus asked Paul why Paul was persecuting *him*. Jesus' connection to the believer is a full union where mutual identities and sufferings are shared.

Along with this shared suffering with Jesus, it has become known throughout the entire "imperial guard" that Paul is on team Jesus. The imperial guard was, in fact, the very group of soldiers who protected the emperor. Think of the guard as the Secret Service. What excites Paul the most is that the gospel is infiltrating the ranks of the emperor who was worshiped as lord. This is a wonderful cause for rejoicing! Regardless of what happens, Paul knows that his suffering has advanced the gospel to the very heart of Roman worship.

Not only that, many other Christians have looked at Paul's imprisonment and have received encouragement from him. These believers have become more confident *in the Lord*, and because of it, they are preaching with boldness. Paul challenged them and they are rising to the occasion. For Paul, this is yet another reason to

---

[13] Frank Thielman, *Philippians*, The NIV Application Commentary (Grand Rapids, MI: Zondervan Publishing House, 1995). 59.

rejoice! The gospel is going forward not only in his ministry, but the ministry of others.

Can it be *that* good, Paul?

> Some indeed preach Christ from envy and rivalry, but others from good will. The latter do it out of love, knowing that I am put here for the defense of the gospel. The former proclaim Christ out of selfish ambition, not sincerely but thinking to afflict me in my imprisonment. What then? Only that in every way, whether in pretense or in truth, Christ is proclaimed, and in that I rejoice.[14]

Apparently not. Even in joy there is suffering; and in suffering, joy.

Some brothers are getting more confident in the Lord and are preaching without fear. Others are preaching out of envy and competition instead. The former are doing it out of love because of the gospel and Paul's ministry going forward. The latter are doing it to try and "afflict" Paul.

Instead of getting discouraged, Paul sees that these people, whomever they are, are preaching Christ. Even if they are trying to mock Paul and make fun of his imprisonment, they are preaching the gospel, and Jesus is getting glory. For Paul, that is all that matters.

These men have been the subject of many books, and I simply cannot get into it at this time. What we do know is that they are preaching the gospel (not a false gospel

---

[14] Phil. 1:15-18b.

like the Judaizers in Galatia). They are simply parting ways from Paul, viewing him as a nonessential to the advancement of the gospel. Were they like pastors of churches today who compete with others to offer the biggest and best programs? Probably not. Regardless, however, Christ is proclaimed "and in that [Paul] [can] rejoice."[15]

HAVING JOY WHEN SUFFERING

Christian: keep in mind that you were saved by suffering. You were set free by defeat. Your salvation came by humiliation. Your justification came by condemnation. Jesus' suffering and subsequent vindication are the basis of your right-standing before God. Never forget this.

Paul's entire worldview centers on a Sovereign God who uses all human circumstances to achieve his gospel ends. Nothing happens apart from God's providential will and sovereign orchestration. This brings sheer joy to the Christian because she can know that no matter the circumstance, God has it under his control. We must do our part to fight for joy during it. When difficult things arise, we must, like Paul, look for ways in which the gospel is going, or can go, forward. Suffering has a way of refining our humanity. It humbles the proud by pointing us to Jesus and from there gives grace to the

---

[15] It is believed that this mockery is what led to Paul's execution. For a fuller treatment on this, see Frank Thielman, *Philippians*, The NIV Application Commentary (Grand Rapids, MI: Zondervan Publishing House, 1995). 58-61.

weary. It always goes back to the gospel.

The theology of glory says that God works in spite of problematic conditions. The theology of the cross says that God works *through* problematic conditions. When our focus is on us and our response, we fail to focus on Christ and his work. Adverse conditions will come and go; only Christ's work lasts forever.

You see, God uses suffering. He does not trivialize it, nor does he vengefully inflict it. He uses it to advance the gospel for it is the gospel that is truly good news. The world says what it does about suffering, but God works in and through it. Fighting for joy requires us not to find delight and joy in our circumstances that change but in the unchanging gospel message. If we lack this joy, we must fight for it, repenting of sin and searching the Scriptures for the truth about God. Remember that the fight for joy is a fight to see, and the fight to see is a fight to savor the infinite beauty of Christ. Like Paul, let us rejoice, *again*, that God has revealed himself in the gospel.

4 - **FACING DEATH**

Yes, and I will rejoice, for I know that through your prayers and the help of the Spirit of Jesus Christ this will turn out for my deliverance, as it is my eager expectation and hope that I will not be at all ashamed, but that with full courage now as always Christ will be honored in my body, whether by life or by death. For to me to live is Christ, and to die is gain. If I am to live in the flesh, that means fruitful labor for me. Yet which I shall choose I cannot tell. I am hard pressed between the two. My desire is to depart and be with Christ, for that is far better. But to remain in the flesh is more necessary on your account. Convinced of this, I know that I will remain and continue with you all, for your progress and joy in the faith, so that in me you may have ample cause to glory in Christ Jesus, because of my coming to you again.

Only let your manner of life be worthy of the gospel of Christ, so that whether I come and see you or am absent, I may hear of you that you are standing firm in one spirit, with one mind striving side by side for the faith of the gospel, and not frightened in anything by your opponents. This is a clear sign to them of their destruction, but of your salvation, and that from God. For it has been granted to you that for the sake of Christ you should not only believe in him but also suffer for his sake, engaged in the same conflict that you saw I had and now hear that I still have.[1]

Ten out of ten people die each year. Regardless of age, skin color or gender, it is inevitable—you will die some day. It is a sobering thought. To think that this life we live will end at some point is virtually unthinkable. My guess is that you do not spend a lot of time thinking about death. Maybe you are reading this on your deathbed, and what I just said is not true for you—you are thinking intensely about it. For the majority of people however, I would argue that it is true: many of us do not sit around thinking about death except for funerals and such. The adage is true: ten out of ten people die each and every year. Since we're on the subject of statistics, I had heard it said once before that over 6,000 people die every hour. Like suffering, it is inescapable and inevitable. How will you handle it?

Personally, I have never had a "near death" experience. My brother has nearly drowned a few times on some canoe trips in northern Michigan, but for me, I do not believe I have ever seen "the light." I recently had my appendix removed (unexpectedly), and that had me a little nervous, but I did not think about dying. I was thinking about my family and asking God to get me fixed. So I am unable, to some extent, to empathize with

[1] Phil. 1:19-30.

you, if "you" are a person who has had such an experience.

Death has a way of sobering us up. It is a quick reality check. I do not know why this is the case, but my guess is that the reason it wakes us up is that it is either fearful, or uncertain. You cannot control it (and we love control). When your time is up, it is up. That is some serious stuff. We do not know what it will be like because we only get the occasion to die once, and then we face judgment (Heb. 9:27). Fear of the unknown is a reality we must wrestle with when it comes to this topic.

I also think that death is scary. I just mentioned fear, but I think *scary* is also an appropriate adjective. While I have not spent considerable time pondering this reality, I have worried about the means by which I might pass into eternity. I think having a heart attack is my biggest fear. (This is because I have had heart palpitations on and off for several years, and it builds up to anxiety and then I begin to get scared). This stuff alarms me. If I can be honest, it scares me to think about leaving my wife and kids behind, and it scares me to think that I will miss them growing up.

Death is the real deal.

THE WAGES OF SIN AND THE GOSPEL

The Bible's story begins with a virtuous God creating all things good. With a desire to know good and evil as only God can know good and evil, Adam and Eve fall into transgression and the result is death.

And the LORD God commanded the man, saying, "You

> may surely eat of every tree of the garden, but of the
> tree of the knowledge of good and evil you shall not eat,
> for in the day that you eat of it you shall surely die.[2]

Innocence was lost, and guilt suddenly imposed. Sin has now taken over, and death has become the new reality.[3]

At some level, the spirit and body, created in unity, became fractured by sin. Disease, sickness and a wicked heart are now the fruit of a sin-tainted soul. Because of this promise, death has intervened where life once stood.

The apostle Paul declares in Romans 6:23 that the "wages of sin is death." Because God's holiness requires a perfect righteousness, the consequence of something unholy and unrighteous is death. Herein lies the ultimate problem begging for an ultimate solution in the gospel. Paul writes early in Romans 3: "All have sinned and fall short of the glory of God" (23). In other words, we were created to extol, praise, give weight to, exult, honor, magnify, glorify, be satisfied in, and treasure God. Sin distorts this reality. Joy has been taken from us and now we must fight to get it back.

I said in the last chapter that Jesus *has saved* us from the *penalty* of sin, *is saving* us from the *power* of sin and *will save* us from the *presence* of sin. Immediately you can see how pivotal a role the gospel plays in the life of a

---

[2] Genesis 2:16-17.

[3] "Therefore, just as sin came into the world through one man, and death through sin, and so death spread to all men because all sinned..." (Rom. 5:12).

believer who is fighting for joy while facing death. Even though our penalty is paid and Christ's righteousness given to us, we are still being refined as the Spirit convicts us of sin and cleanses us from all unrighteousness (see 1 Jn. 1:9ff.). Death is still a reality, and while its sting is removed because of a redemptive future (1 Cor. 15:55), it is still something we must face. Only when Jesus appears to consummate his kingdom will the final piece of the gospel be put in place. We must be removed from the presence of sin if we are to do away with death—and this is what we wait for with eager hope (Rom. 8:24).

What the Bible makes abundantly clear over and over again is that God is at work in his creation. Scripture says that the wages of sin is death, but God does not give up nor is he away on a cosmic vacation. He is active inside his creation, wooing his beings to come and drink deep from the gospel spring. Because this is his character and propensity, God is not scared of death; instead he enters into our condemnation and sin by dying in our place, for our sins.

A CONTINUING THOUGHT

What I hope to do in this chapter is connect the dots as we look at Philippians 1:18b-30 as it pertains to death. What is essential to notice right away is that this section is not to be taken in isolation. Paul has just talked about his loneliness in prison, and how gospel partnership has helped him in the fight for joy. Because of his relationship with the beloved church, Paul handles this loneliness by being reminded of them always in his prayers for their progress in the faith and their advancement of the gospel in partnership with him. Though they are far away in terms of proximity, they are near because of their bond in the Spirit and common goal rooted in Jesus Christ.

Not only this, he has led us into his experience of suffering by reminding us that we are saved *through* suffering. Paul is a gospel-centered man and he has a robust theology of the cross that refuses to leave him with questions as to why he is suffering, but instead praises God continually, regardless of what happens.

Both of these sections are *present* evaluations. Paul is giving his church an update on how things are going *now*. In this next section, while a continuing thought pattern, Paul is looking forward. He is going to invite us to look into the future to learn how to fight for joy when facing death.

HONOR HIM!

To begin, God demands worship. This sounds incredibly odd, and almost makes God sound like an insecure person who is vying for compliments. He is not. God does not *need* your praise and honor any more than he *needs* your advice. Because God is the greatest good in the universe, it follows that he ought to be worshiped. Since he holds the position of highest honor and supremacy, his creation ought to give him back what is his, namely, praise. If we value something, we praise it. Whether it is a hamburger at the local greasy spoon, or a football player, we take pleasure in taking pleasure in something of value. C.S. Lewis once said (and I'm paraphrasing), that it is the way everything works in the world, and that *praising* something is the ultimate end of *delighting* in something. In other words, you do not fully enjoy that hamburger unless you tell someone about it and rejoice with words and affections. Since God is of ultimate worth and supreme value, we are to praise him, not because he lacks confidence, but because it is for *our good*. Anything less than God is an idol, and idols are harmful.

Look at what some of the Psalms tell (command) us regarding the magnification of God:

> Oh, magnify the LORD with me, and let us exalt his name together! (34:3)

> Let those who delight in my righteousness shout for joy and be glad and say forevermore, "Great is the LORD, who delights in the welfare of his servant!" (35:27)

> But may all who seek you rejoice and be glad in you; may those who love your salvation say continually, "Great is the LORD!" (40:16)

> Be exalted, O God, above the heavens! Let your glory be over all the earth! (57:11)

> I will praise the name of God with a song; I will magnify him with thanksgiving. (69:30)

> May all who seek you rejoice and be glad in you! May those who love your salvation say evermore, "God is great!" (70:4)

> How great are your works, O LORD! Your thoughts are very deep! (92:5)

> Bless the LORD, O my soul! O LORD my God, you are very great! You are clothed with splendor and majesty. (104:1)

> O LORD, how manifold are your works! In wisdom have you made them all; the earth is full of your creatures. (104:24)

> Then our mouth was filled with laughter, and our tongue with shouts of joy; then they said among the nations, "The LORD has done great things for them." The LORD has done great things for us; we are glad. (126:2-3)

God is most glorified in us when we are most satisfied in him. He takes pleasure in being God. He takes pleasure in giving us pleasure in himself. Notice that, in each of these circumstances, the unfathomable truths about God promote verbal worship and in turn, verbal worship promotes a response. This cycle fosters intimate reflection on God. It is a mutual process of the magnification of God in worship. God reveals something astonishing about himself, and we respond to him, and vice versa.

This is how Paul starts his argument in this section: "honor him." In other words, like a telescope, magnify, extol and give glory to God *through* your life.

THE TEXT

Paul begins this section:

> Yes, and I will rejoice, for I know that through your prayers and the help of the Spirit of Jesus Christ this will turn out for my deliverance, as it is my eager expectation and hope that I will not be at all ashamed, but that with full courage now as always Christ will be honored in my body, whether by life or by death.[4]

As mentioned previously, the apostle moves from his present circumstances (his imprisonment and subsequent gospel fruit), to a future evaluation. At the center of this transition is the phrase, "Yes, and I will rejoice." He just praised God that Christ has been made *known* through his imprisonment (1:13). He also rejoices that Christ is *preached* despite his critics trying to heap infirmity on him (1:18). Now Paul rejoices yet again because even though he is facing death, Christ will be *honored* (1:20).

For Paul, the worst in life has happened and the only thing left for him would be death. Through it all he chose to value Christ above all and in doing so, found joy in all circumstances and trials.

There are several key words in the section that we must deal with in order to understand where Paul is going. The first word is *deliverance*. Paul says that with the help of the prayers of the Philippians, and the

---

[4] Phil. 1:18b-20.

simultaneous presence of the Spirit,[5] he will be delivered (*soteria*). The word he uses here usually refers to the vindication and salvation that one would receive on the final day of God's judgment. While this is Paul's ultimate vision, he is also hoping to be delivered from prison (1:25). What is curious about Paul's phraseology here is that in the Greek text of the Old Testament,[6] Paul quotes from Job 13:16 verbatim. In this section of the book, Job is claiming with absolute certainty that God will vindicate him when he stands before the judgment seat despite his unhelpful friends. Whether Paul intentionally means to echo this verse or not is besides the point (I think he does). God's salvation on the last day is what Paul expects, and nothing can deter his hope and "full courage." He know that God vindicates the righteous.

The second word we need to analyze is the word *ashamed* (*aischynomai*). When we think of someone feeling shame or being ashamed, we typically define it in terms of disgrace or dishonor. This is not at all what the Bible means when it uses this terminology. What the Bible means by this word is more of what we would think of with the word disappointment. What Paul is getting at is that he will not find disappointment if his trust is in the right place, that is to say, in God. Paul

---

[5] "Help" in this sentence is not the best translation. "Gift," "presence," or "supply" of the Spirit would be what Paul intends to mean here. It is the gift of the Spirit from God in fresh supply (cf. Gal. 3:5).

[6] Called the Septuagint (LXX).

understands that if death comes his way, he will not be disappointed because he will see Christ. If he continues on in life, Christ will be honored (magnified) and even then, he will not be disappointed because of the hope found in the gospel. In this sense, through the gospel, there is no such thing as disappointment.

To extrapolate even further, Paul uses this language in Romans 1:16, by saying that he is "not ashamed of the gospel, because it is the power of God for salvation." There is power in the gospel that keeps the Christian from despair and disillusionment.

Part of the reason that Paul has this confidence is because Jesus has been exalted to the highest rank of Lordship in the universe. No one can defeat him—not even death! Coupled with this belief was his understanding that Christ would be magnified *in him*. Remember that Paul told the Philippian church the same thing in verse 6 of chapter 1: "He who began a good work in you will bring it to completion at the day of Jesus Christ." Disappointment is simply not an option for Paul; not when Christ is all!

Another phrase Paul employs that requires some further examination is his view of Christ being magnified "in [his] body." We know from 1 Cor. 10:31 that we are to glorify God in all things, whether we eat or drink. The reason Paul can say that Christ will be glorified in his body is because God dwells within him and no matter what happens, God will be using it to achieve his gospel ends (see Chapter 3 above). When Christians use whatever circumstances that comes her way, she can glorify God in her body by acknowledging that God is at work within her (Phil. 2:13). You and I cannot "be Jesus" to someone (that job is taken). Nevertheless, we can display with our head, heart and hands that Jesus is Lord and that the gospel means something. (Hence Paul's entire situation!) Magnifying, honoring, and exalting God requires not only orthodoxy (right belief), but orthopraxy (right practice), too. When we give weight to God and what he has done in Christ, and subsequently live in light of this astounding truth, we honor him.

Paul goes on:

> For to me to live is Christ, and to die is gain. If I am to live in the flesh, that means fruitful labor for me. Yet which I shall choose I cannot tell. I am hard pressed between the two. My desire is to depart and be with Christ, for that is far better. But to remain in the flesh is more necessary on your account. Convinced of this, I know that I will remain and continue with you all, for your progress and joy in the faith, so that in me you may have ample cause to glory in Christ Jesus, because of my coming to you again.[7]

What rings through loud and clear in this letter over and over again is that Paul loves this church *deeply*. He loves them enough to forgo heaven so that their faith in the Christ can be cultivated. Amazing.

"For to me to live is Christ, and to die is gain." This verse has always been one of my favorites. It is often

---

[7] Phil. 1:21-26.

quoted out of noble intent, but is a subject of controversy to Western Christians because living here is not always about Christ alone. Nonetheless, this verse is incredibly powerful. What is certain is that death cannot be gain unless Christ is treasured in your life, *here and now.* Let me explain.

The American dream (however you might define it) is something that Christians live and die for. Ask yourself the question, for to me to live is _____? For what reasons are you living? Paul was thoroughly blown away by God's grace in Christ and was willing to sacrifice *everything* for him. Is this your attitude? If Christ enough for you?

Christ is the center of Christianity. If you remove Christ, you have nothing. He is the deciding factor for all things. Many will not join a church for numerous reasons; giving no serious consideration to whom Christ is and what he would have for that person in the local church. We fight and argue over petty issues without Jesus at the center, giving us eyes to see. Paul's life was deeply gospel-saturated. For example, he writes, "I have been crucified with Christ. It is no longer I who live, but Christ who lives in me. And the life I now live in the flesh I live by faith in the Son of God, who loved me and gave himself for me" (Gal. 2:20). Anything that Paul has in life he considers rubbish (Phil. 3:8). Christ is truly all. Where is your faith? Where is your fellowship? Are you a genuine follower of Jesus? These are tough questions.

But how is death gain? Simply put, death is gain because Christ is our treasure and to be with Christ in his presence is far greater than anything the world has to offer (1:23). The phrase Paul uses in this verse brings lucidity in the Greek. Paul says that to live is *Christos* and to die is *kerdos*. The two words rhyme and are meant to play off of one another. While in our culture death is oftentimes glorified,[8] Paul is not using it so he can escape from this world, but instead enter through death with Christ so that he can be *in Christ*. (To be sure, he is "in Christ" and his theology reflects it). To die is of ultimate gain because Christ is ultimate.

What is unfortunate about people's view of this world and death is the Platonic dualism that is perpetuated by the likes of dispensationalists and Semi-Pelagian Christians. For many believers, this life is just an awful reality to escape from and that some day God is going to zap all the Christians off of the planet (a concept entirely foreign to the Bible). They believe that death is gain because this life is unspeakable (do you hear the theology of glory?) and that we only need a way out. Wrong. Dead wrong. Paul does not view this life as horrendous. He does not see death as a release from a life of suffering. "Death for the Christian is never pictured in the Bible as gain over the worst in this life. Instead it is portrayed as an improvement on the best."[9] Though he suffered, Paul's life was centered on Jesus, and this was sufficient for him. Are there benefits from

---

[8] In other words, we are fascinated with it; we love movies that push us to the limit.

[9] James Montgomery Boice, *Philippians: An Expositional Commentary* (Grand Rapids, MI: Baker Books, 2000). 81.

death? Absolutely. For the Christian, we get to be with Jesus, free from the evil in this world. But Paul is not wanting to die for the sake of escape. He is ready to see his savior in all of his fullness—an opportunity that will happen either by death or Christ's appearance.

While this is true, Paul goes on to talk about his ambivalent feelings towards the future. Yes, he wants to be with Christ in his glory, but he wants to continue on in gospel proclamation, helping the Philippian church grow in their joy and faith (1:25). In saying this, he puts the needs of the Philippian church over his own.

Finishing out chapter 1, Paul writes:

> Only let your manner of life be worthy of the gospel of Christ, so that whether I come and see you or am absent, I may hear of you that you are standing firm in one spirit, with one mind striving side by side for the faith of the gospel, and not frightened in anything by your opponents. This is a clear sign to them of their destruction, but of your salvation, and that from God. For it has been granted to you that for the sake of Christ you should not only believe in him but also suffer for his sake, engaged in the same conflict that you saw I had and now hear that I still have.[10]

As Paul reflects on his future, he also exhorts the Philippians in their future. When facing death, Paul does not murmur or undermine the sovereignty of God; no, he goes back to work in the fight for joy.

---

[10] Phil. 1:27-30.

Paul encourages the Philippians to "let [their} manner of life be worthy" of the gospel. The word used here is *politeuo*, and it is connected the noun *polis*, which is where we get the word "city". What Paul is saying is better translated as "live as citizens" in gospel community. Paul is not talking about an actual city, but rather the Church, the City of God. We are members of the body of Christ, and we are to act like it by striving together in the unity of spirit and mind, working hard together to see the gospel advance. If we can act in unity (though diverse), this will inevitably lead to striving together for the gospel.

E. Stanley Jones helps us:

> The early Christians did not say in dismay: 'Look what the world has come to,' but in delight, 'Look what has come to the world.' They saw not merely the ruin, but the resources for the reconstruction of that ruin. They saw not merely that sin did abound, but that grace did much more abound. On that assurance the pivot of history swung from blank despair, loss of moral nerve, and fatalism, to faith and confidence that at last sin had met its match, that something new had come into the world, that not only here and there, but on a wide scale, men could attain to that hitherto impossible thing—goodness.[11]

It would be far too easy to look at the world and

---

[11] E. Stanley Jones, *Abundant Living* (Nashville, TN: Abingdon Press, 1942), 183. Quoted in James Montgomery Boice, *Philippians: An Expositional Commentary* (Grand Rapids, MI: Baker Books, 2000). 90.

discount its goodness. As one who holds to the doctrine of total depravity, I also hold to the position that the creator God has a purpose in redemption through the glorious hope found in the gospel. And this, I believe, is what Paul supposes, too. He says that the church will suffer at the hands of their opponents. However, their suffering and persistence in the fight for joy will be a sign of defeat for their opponents, and a sign salvation for the church.

Paul's theology of the cross shows up again when he says that for the sake of Christ, we must all suffer, and indeed shall. That is what it means to be cruciform—or, cross-shaped; it means to be crucified *with* Christ and to fill up in his afflictions (Col. 1:24). As the Philippian church strives together in unity, they will suffer, for their purpose is not of this world, though it has everything to do with the world. The gospel *must* prevail, and indeed it *will* prevail. Suffering and death is simply a means to a God-exalting end.

THE FIGHT FOR JOY: FACING DEATH

There is much to be said about this section and to do so would require another book. But I want to close out this chapter with a few more thoughts.

To start, there is plenty for us to learn from this passage.

We can learn about the centrality of the Spirit in the fight for joy, and how the Spirit can and will strongly come upon the believer in times of suffering. Why else would Paul depend on the prayers of the Philippian church for a fresh supply of the Spirit when he already possesses him? Do you pray for those who are suffering and facing death to experience the Spirit in a fresh way? In short: we have an underdeveloped pneumatology, and we could learn a lot from Paul's doctrine of the Holy Spirit.

We can also learn a lot from Paul on what it means to stare death in the face and still choose life for the sake of the gospel. While many would love to just opt-out of life so that they can "go to heaven" when they die, Paul sets an example here in this text for us to remember our calling to be gospel partners whose lives are captivated by the mission of God.

I could go on and on about the Christian life being sorrowful, yet always rejoicing; walking through suffering yet fighting for joy because we were bought with a price through suffering. The reality is this text comes down to a couple of crucial things.

First, are you submerged in the depths of the gospel? Are you *tasting* and *seeing* that the Lord is good (Ps. 34:8)? Is your life entranced with a vision of God that is so gigantic, that you can stare death in the face, groan for the fullness of Christ, and yet turn it away so that you can be about the mission? Is the gospel enough for you? Or are you running on the performance treadmill hoping to impress God?

The mission is the second part. The mission is to make disciples, and Paul has fully sold himself to it. Where are you in this? Are you a part of a gospel community on mission? Are you able to assess your life accurately, and re-engineer it around the mission of God? Or has the comforts of the American dream swallowed you up? The fight for joy facing death encapsulates these two things. You may be suffering, and you may be unsure about the future—but what is your focus? The gospel? Let it be so. "Precious in the sight of the LORD is the death of his saints" (Ps. 116:15). If we must die, let us get Christ. If we must live, let it be for Christ.

5 - WITH HUMILITY

So if there is any encouragement in Christ, any comfort from love, any participation in the Spirit, any affection and sympathy, complete my joy by being of the same mind, having the same love, being in full accord and of one mind. Do nothing from selfish ambition or conceit, but in humility count others more significant than yourselves. Let each of you look not only to his own interests, but also to the interests of others. Have this mind among yourselves, which is yours in Christ Jesus, who, though he was in the form of God, did not count equality with God a thing to be grasped, but emptied himself, by taking the form of a servant, being born in the likeness of men. And being found in human form, he humbled himself by becoming obedient to the point of death, even death on a cross. Therefore God has highly exalted him and bestowed on him the name that is above every name, so that at the name of Jesus every knee should bow, in heaven and on earth and under the earth, and every tongue confess that Jesus Christ is Lord, to the glory of God the Father.[1]

---

[1] Phil. 2:1-11.

Humility is somewhat of a lost cause in our society of self-fulfillment and self-actualization. The crescendo of human achievement as it stands in the American West is *self*. From the plethora of self-help books, to New Year's resolutions—everyone is on a mission of self, and that self is all that matters. I define this notion of self-improvement as anything we do to make ourselves morally better. There is no gospel, just "do." Work harder, make more money, get a bigger house, try harder, do better, think clearer, run faster, diet more, and try to be patient in traffic. All of these are noble goals, but they are impossible without the work of the Holy Spirit applying the gospel of Jesus to your head, heart and hands.

It has been said that humility is something that when you think you have it, you basically do not. It is incredibly shy and leaves the room when talked about. I have also heard it said that humility is not thinking less of yourself, but instead, it is thinking of your self, less. In other words, it is not the pursuit of self-demeaning behavior as though we should beat ourselves up into some sort of moral submission. Nor is it the false humility of pretending as though you care about someone else. No, it is putting the needs of others before your own and by doing so, it frees you from the grip of pride and self-interest. At its origin, humility can only be assessed when you look upon the holiness of God, and the sinfulness of your sin—only then can you see yourself as you truly are.

Pride is a sin that frequents the human heart. It

shows up inside of our minds when we elevate ourselves above others. It shows up in our hearts when conspire evil against someone or choose to believe the lie instead of the truth about God. It shows up in our hands when we cut someone off on the road because what we have going on is more urgent than whatever it is those "slow pokes" are doing. Pride is destructive as the book of Proverbs so clearly lays out:

> The fear of the LORD is hatred of evil. Pride and arrogance and the way of evil and perverted speech I hate (8:13).

> When pride comes, then comes disgrace, but with the humble is wisdom (11:2).

> Pride goes before destruction, and a haughty spirit before a fall (16:18).

> "Scoffer" is the name of the arrogant, haughty man who acts with arrogant pride (21:24).

> One's pride will bring him low, but he who is lowly in spirit will obtain honor (29:23).

1 John 2:16 says, "For all that is in the world—the desires of the flesh and the desires of the eyes and pride in possessions—is not from the Father but is from the world." Jesus echoes the Scripture's position on the matter:

> Do you not see that whatever goes into a person from

outside cannot defile him, since it enters not his heart, but his stomach, and is expelled? (Thus he declared all foods clean.) And he said, "What comes out of a person is what defiles him. For from within, out of the heart of man, come evil thoughts, sexual immorality, theft, murder, adultery, coveting, wickedness, deceit, sensuality, envy, slander, *pride*, foolishness. All these evil things come from within, and they defile a person."[2]

Pride is devastation, and her father is iniquity. If we as Christians are to fight for joy, we must do so with humility, but not just with *our* humility (which oftentimes is a false humility), but with Christ's humility. Fighting for joy is fight against pride and her fruit as we see and savor Jesus Christ.

I would like to pause for a moment and come back to this issue of humility after dealing with some other affairs.

SOME CONCERNS

Something that concerns me with churchgoers, and I'm writing this with some of those in mind that are a part of our community, is that we have, to be straightforward, an impotent view of the gospel. Many folks have reduced the gospel to a crutch of self-moralization, and worse yet, some have posited Jesus to be just another thought to think from time-to-time without regard to his personhood and presence inside of the believer.

---

[2] Mark 7:18-23, emphasis mine.

Those who have this utterly powerless, impotent and small gospel view will have a powerless, impotent and small Christian life. If Jesus is not on the throne in heaven as Lord *here and now*, then your life will not look that way. So many people "attend" church, and that is the real problem—our gospel identity suffers.[3] The gospel has been reduced to a powerless concept and a powerless Lord who is unable to change his/her life. The problem is not God it is you and me. Christianity is not first and foremost an activity of the subjugated will, it is an identity. It contains activities, yes, but that is not the starting point. (The starting point is Jesus' activity!) Part of my job as a preacher is to remind my people of whom God is, and who they are in light of his character. If we fall into the trap of the impotent gospel we will default to therapeutic moralistic deism, and sadly this is what many have done.

The other concern that I have is that we have a truncated view of the gospel to go alongside our impotent view of the gospel. Not only is it powerless, but it is shortened. Here's what I mean: If we see the Christian life as simply one activity we do on a Sunday instead of an identity to live within (and then make disciples), then we have a shortened version of the gospel and we need more gospel. These folks want forgiveness without having to love their neighbor. They want heaven without mission here. They want to escape hell and not have to work real hard while on earth. They

---

[3] No one in history has ever attended church.

want a friendly Jesus but not a Lord that requires them to bow down before him. Simply put: they have castrated their gospel by belittling its significance, depth and (eventually) truth.

The theological ineptitude of many Christians is simply astounding. Doctrine has become something for only the "nerds," and holiness is dumbed down to a movement of Jesus freaks back in the sixties. I recently had a conversation with some local pastors at our monthly ministerial association meeting. In that conversation, I was told about a gentleman who came into one of the churches looking for answers because he wanted to "rededicate" his life back to Jesus. My Arminian friend joked and said, "See, Jason: 'rededicate'." (We often banter on about theology, poking fun with each other. I love it.) After he concluded his statement, I replied, "Truthfully, he needs a regenerated heart. He needs to get saved the first time." While this was said in jest, I certainly was convinced by my statement. We dilly-dally with doctrine and end up with terrible theology that leads to abysmal Christian living. If we are not *crystal clear* (as much as possible) on our theology, we will see the de-churched numbers increase as well as see our precious "attendance" decrease. We simply cannot afford to have a gospel that is incoherent and incompetent. Doctrine unequivocally matters.

Now, having said all of that, you are probably wondering how this connects with humility and pride. Please read on.

THE TEXT

I want to jump right in to the text in this chapter because there is much to discuss.

> So if there is any encouragement in Christ, any comfort from love, any participation in Spirit, any affection and sympathy, complete my joy by being of the same mind, having the same love, being in full accord and of one mind. Do nothing from rivalry or conceit, but in humility count others more significant than yourselves. Let each of you look not only to his own interests, but also to the interests of others.[4]

This section should not been seen as separate from the previous verses in 1:27-30. There is an ongoing thought as Paul reflected on his, as well as their suffering and opponents (1:28); he now focuses on any internal dissension happening within the church (which apparently there was some of this going on; see, for example, 4:2).

Previously, Paul instructed his beloved church to live a life in such a way that is worthy of the gospel. We are to live life as citizens of a greater kingdom—one that will never fade away. Then he moves into some profound reflection. He states that there are certain things that we get in Christ. We get encouragement, namely, the "iron-sharpens-iron" that happens when the body of Christ functions in unity. We get comfort from Christ's love and are able to extend it to the other (don't forget

---

[4] Phil. 2:1-4.

that the Holy Spirit is called the *Comforter*). We also have a participation (*koinonia*) in the Spirit, a bond that cannot be broken. In the gospel, we also get affection and sympathy (literally, "tenderness and compassion") because of Jesus. Consequently, as Paul sees the depths of the gospel, he rhetorically reminds the church that these things *are* true, and if they are true, then there is something more to life than just receiving these gifts: *they are to do something with them.*

This "something" is to use those gifts to complete Paul's joy (they are his "joy and crown" in 4:1) by (1) being of the same mind, (2) having the same love, and (3) being of one accord and one mind. For Paul unity, notwithstanding diversity, is his theological dream for the church. He knows there is diversity in his congregation. He started with a rich woman, formerly demon-possessed slave girl, and a Roman jailer! Even still, the church is called to be united, and we do so by putting the needs of others ahead of our own. His exhortation is strong: "Do nothing from rivalry or conceit" (2:3). In other words, "Don't be prideful. There's no room for this! Do not be arrogant! Be humble! Do not just look out for your own needs," Paul says, "Look at your neighbor and count him as more significant than yourself."

Shocking.

Pride will ruin any relationship. It is what earned Satan a removal from heaven (Is. 14:12-15). If you are only going to look out for yourself, then yourself is all you will have in the end. Pride is destructive, and it will annihilate a local church. If you claim to follow Jesus and do not put others before yourself, you are following your self and not Jesus.

Now, I could do you a complete disservice and end this section by saying, "OK, guys, do this." "Just do it," would be the application, and I could make you feel good and inspired to go and do this command for unity and humility. It would work for about a day. "Just think better thoughts and declare today your day," says the prosperity preachers. This is not gospel-centrality, not at even close! I would be a fool to leave you there. This is not what Paul does. He does not say to us, "Here, go and be humble. Good luck. Be moral, think better thoughts, and try to love someone today." That is not the gospel. Paul would be entirely exasperated by this conclusion.

For Paul, every imperative (command) is united to an indicative (truth about God). He will never tell you only to go and do better. He will never just say to you, "Be humble!" For Paul, remember, the gospel takes primacy in all things. Doctrine matters because doctrine is how we learn about God. When we learn about God, we can live in light of whom he is. We must have gospel before law, the indicative before the imperative.

Paul tells us to have the same attitude that Jesus had. He connects the command to fight for joy with humility by learning from Jesus and how he fought for joy:

> Have this mind among yourselves, which is yours in Christ Jesus, who, thought he was in the form of God, did not count equality with God a thing to be grasped, but made himself nothing, taking the form of a servant, being born in the likeness of men. And being found in

human form, he humbled himself by becoming obedient to the point of death, even death on a cross.[5]

Paul says four things about Jesus in this section, and we will start with this:

1. Jesus thought of others, not just himself.

The command is to have the same mind (attitude) which is ours "in Christ Jesus." In other words, yes, we are called to be humble by warring against pride and cultivating humility. The pattern is not moralistic do-good-ism. The pattern is outlined by Jesus, and to start, Jesus thought of others before himself.

This section of Scripture has been the subject of many books throughout history. Many scholars believe that Paul quotes this as an early Christian hymn and that he was not the original author. True or not, and I think it was early and originated somewhere else, it has a creedal flavor to it and boldly speaks the truth about Jesus the GodMan.

Paul says that Jesus was the "form of God." In other words, Jesus was and is God (cf. John 1:1ff) and has eternally existed as the Second Person of the Trinity. This is Paul's way of contrasting Jesus' deity with the fact that he also took on the "form" of a servant (1:7). What is pertinent to note here is that this verse, amongst many others in the New Testament, gives

---

[5] Phil. 2:5-8.

weight to the truth that Jesus has always existed as a part of the Trinitarian Godhead; he is God incarnate.

This is our second point found in this section:

2. Jesus Serves.

Paul says that Jesus did not count equality with God a thing to be grasped. Stated differently, Jesus did not have a haughty view of himself that said he should hang on to his rights and power as God and exploit them. Jesus did not hang on so tightly to his deity that he failed to achieve the mission that he was sent to do; no, he "emptied himself," by laying those rights aside so that he could take on true humanity in order to efficaciously atone for sin. Jesus didn't seize to be God, for that would be impossible; he merely relinquished his status in heaven, and he took on the form of a servant, or "slave," making himself a "nobody." Jesus came to serve, not to be served (Mt. 20:28; cf. Is. 42:1).

At the incarnation, Jesus added humanity to his divinity. Though perfectly God, he became human, and though he did not sin (2 Cor. 5:21), he was tempted in every way (Heb. 4:15) and remained inculpable. Jesus Christ condescended to rescue us, and this hypostatic union is fundamental to Christian doctrine.[6]

The third thing Paul asserts:

3. Jesus Sacrifices.

---

[6] "Hypostatic union" refers to Jesus being fully God and full man.

Paul says that Jesus was found in human form and "humbled himself," by becoming obedient to the Father, even while journeying to the cross. Jesus' obedience to the Father was vital to his mission. Throughout the book of John, he says that he has come to glorify the Father (Jn. 7:18; 8:50, 54; 11:4; 17:5, 22, 24). He obeys what the Father has told him to do, and the Father affirms him (Mk. 1:11). His obedience led him to the cross, where the penalty for sin was laid upon him, and the true sacrificial lamb was slain.

This verse does not shock us when we read it. We are so accustomed the commercialization of the cross that we are numb to the horror of what it represents. The cross was a murderous symbol of torture. Only the worst of law-breakers were crucified. Roman citizens were not to be crucified unless the emperor himself gave consent. Jesus' hands and feet were nailed with the large Roman nails to the cross and there he died, naked and alone. The cross is scandalous. May we never lose sight of its weight, significance, depths and beauty. If you are not stunned by what Jesus has done for you on the cross, you will not be humble, for who can be arrogant standing by the cross?

This past week I read an online article from a newspaper that was about a pastor and his ministry. One of this pastor's critics was interviewed about the other guy's position on God's anger towards sin. He said that he does not see how God could be mad at sin, and that it is not the God he reads about in the Bible. I was horrified by this statement. If I could have just a few short minutes of this critic's time, I would say to him, "Then what was the cross? Was it just an accident? Was Jesus simply at the wrong place at the wrong time? Was he just caught up in a mishap in the ever-so-unstable political climate of the first century?"

Of course, it was not an mishap. It was part of the predestined will of the Father (Acts 2:23). The cross should never be minimized, for it is where the wrath and mercy of God collide into a beautiful display of God's glory. God is unquestionably wrathful against sinners (Ps. 5:5), and his justice requires a righteous payment; but he is also merciful. This is the beauty of the cross! His wrath was poured out on Jesus so that he remains just; his mercy was poured out because it is God who offers himself. Man incurred the fine and owed a debt, but could not pay. God could pay the debt with his perfect Son though he did not owe: this is our God! This is the great exchange.

I think there is another layer to this section of Scripture: *If following Jesus has not cost you anything, it is not Jesus you are following.* Paul gives the command to be humble, and he says that this humility is ours "in Christ Jesus," who is the perfect example.[7] When Paul says to have this mind, he means, "Go and die as Jesus did." The pursuit of Jesus as disciples is a call to take up the cross and follow Jesus (Mk. 8:34). This is not a comfortable life.

---

[7] When the Bible speaks of something as an example, it is not merely a cognitive thing, but a participatory thing. In other words, Jesus is not just an abstract example, he is our Lord. And we are in him, therefore since we have his righteousness, we can be humble with the help of the Spirit.

It is a life characterized by suffering and joy, just like Jesus. Following Jesus into the world will cost you something. What has it cost you?

The fourth and final thing that Paul gives us:

4. Jesus gives God glory.

Paul writes:

Therefore God has highly exalted him and bestowed on him the name that is above every name, so that at the name of Jesus every knee should bow, in heaven and on earth and under the earth, and every tongue confess that Jesus Christ is Lord, to the glory of God the Father.[8]

Because of Jesus' substitutionary death and obedience to the Father, God vindicated the Son at his resurrection (1 Tim. 3:16). Following his resurrection, Jesus ascended back to the Father and was seated at the right hand of God, thus earning him the kingdom and title "Lord" (Acts 1:9; cf. Dan. 7:13-14 and 1 Cor. 15:20-28). Whether Paul wrote this or not, the writer obviously had Isaiah 45 in mind, which says that God is all, and Christ is all and that the Lord's name will be made famous in all of the earth. The only appropriate response to hearing the name of Jesus (Lord) is to bend the knee. Either you do so now by confessing his name, or you will be forced to bend your knee at the final Judgment. All of this is for God's glory, Paul declares.

---

[8] Phil. 2:9-11.

God's glory is the infinite worth and majestic holiness of God that is displayed most vividly at the cross of Christ. It is God's majestic transcendence and immanent grace. The worth of God is God's glory, and it is of utmost value. Jesus does all of this in humility, and then is exalted all for God's glory. The Trinity at work in concert for the salvation of man, and the glory of God. Amazing.

SWEET VS. BITTER

If we start with the premise that the chief end of man is to glorify God by enjoying him forever, then it only follows that in order to fight for joy, delight, and happiness in God, we must war against pride. We can war against pride when we realize that we have a greater-than-anything treasure in Jesus. The Church should be filled with pleasure-in-God-seekers. Do that, and you do not have time for pride.

When we bask in the glory of God shown in the face of Christ, we are enamored. It gives us a reality check. When we repent of pride with the help of the Spirit, we can cultivate humility because of Christ's humility. You can consider your neighbor more important than yourself because Christ has stooped low in humility to serve you. This alone should humble us before God.

Thomas Watson said, "Christ is never sweet till sin is felt to be bitter; nor is he rest till man feels sin to be a burden."[9] May we fight for joy with a greater delight in

---

[9] Thomas Watson, *Puritan Gems*, ed. John Adey (London: J. Snow and Ward, 1850), 15.

Christ's humility.

6 - IN THE WORLD, WITH OTHERS

Therefore, my beloved, as you have always obeyed, so now, not only as in my presence but much more in my absence, work out your own salvation with fear and trembling, for it is God who works in you, both to will and to work for his good pleasure.

Do all things without grumbling or disputing, that you may be blameless and innocent, children of God without blemish in the midst of a crooked and twisted generation, among whom you shine as lights in the world, holding fast to the word of life, so that in the day of Christ I may be proud that I did not run in vain or labor in vain. Even if I am to be poured out as a drink offering upon the sacrificial offering of your faith, I am glad and rejoice with you all. Likewise you also should be glad and rejoice with me.

I hope in the Lord Jesus to send Timothy to you soon, so that I too may be cheered by news of you. For I have no one like him, who will be genuinely concerned for your welfare. For they all seek their own interests, not those of Jesus Christ. But you know Timothy's proven worth, how as a son with a father he has served with me in the gospel. I hope therefore to send him just as soon as I see how it will go with me, and I trust in the Lord that shortly I myself will come also.

I have thought it necessary to send to you Epaphroditus my brother and fellow worker and fellow soldier, and your messenger and minister to my need, for he has been longing for you all and has been distressed because you heard that he was ill. Indeed he was ill, near to death. But God had mercy on him, and not only on him but on me also, lest I should have sorrow upon sorrow. I am the more eager to send him, therefore, that you may rejoice at seeing him again, and that I may be less anxious. So receive him in the Lord with all joy, and honor such men, for he nearly died for the work of Christ, risking his life to complete what was lacking in your service to me.[1]

Notice that the title of this chapter says, "In the world, with others," and not "In the world with others." There is a reason that I have chosen to insert the comma where I have. The reason for doing this is because I wanted not just to emphasize "others," in the context of the world, but emphasize *both* as they work together. Put differently, we are to function in the world in community, but there is still an individual element to it. This may seem incredibly pedantic however, the context of the passage demands it to be so, I believe.

Let me illustrate the point even further before we

---

[1] Phil. 2:12-30

jump right into the text.

Many proponents of the biblical doctrine of predestination have debated over whether or not God elects individuals to salvation, or does he do it corporately. In other words, does God just elect a group of people (Israel, Church) or does he elect individuals (Abraham, David, Jesus, You, Me)?

The answer is, yes.

He does both.

The same goes for the section that confronts us in this chapter. Paul understands both the individual effort of the Christian as he lives a life of holiness, as well as the corporate effort of the local church as it pertains to living exemplary lives in a world heavily damaged by sin. It requires a personal holiness and active pursuit of Jesus as an individual, on top of a corporate holiness established in community.

To be sure, these things ought never to be kept in isolation. In other words, the individual is never meant to be in isolation, and the community's DNA is the makeup of the individuals within her. The two work together in a mutual dance of brilliance.

One more thing must be said by way of preface: theology in community is at the heart of the New Testament. It is in the local church where theology is to be done. Oftentimes we think of theology as something that we do individually, or as a small group, and usually it is more of an objective study rather than a Spirit-shaped experience carried out together. Theology is not just a subject to be studied—it is a life to be lived out in the context of gospel communities on mission (more on this later). Having set the stage, let's let Paul take us from here on out:

> Therefore, my beloved, as you have always obeyed, so now, not only as in my presence but much more in my absence, work out your own salvation with fear and trembling, for it is God who works in you, both to will and to work for his good pleasure.[2]

THE DOCTRINE OF SALVATION

Notice that Paul does *not* say, "Work *for* your own salvation," or "Work *to* your own salvation." He does not say, "Work *in* your own salvation," either. In the context of the local church, Paul is urging the individual to work *out* this salvation because God has already worked it in. It is by faith we are justified, and by faith we work towards holiness.

Sometimes these verses are grossly misused and taken out of context. Not only that, the issue of how salvation works has been vehemently debated since the time of Paul. How does one become a Christian? Does faith happen first? Just what order do things happen in so that someone can become a Christian? This is a massively complex question, but I believe that the Bible is quite clear on how salvation works. Yes, it is a mystery, and I do not wish to suggest that I have it all figured out. But on the other hand, we do have a Bible and we can use it and understand this mystery a little more.

---

[2] Phil. 2:12-13.

The doctrine of salvation is incredibly important. It is significant because salvation is weighty. We want people to know Jesus and inherit eternal life. We want people to find deep and abiding joy in Jesus, and some day spend eternity with him in the New Heavens and New Earth. So we have to be careful talking about this, and remember to be as biblical as possible.

To start, we were created for God's glory (Is. 43:7). When God started his creation project, Adam and Eve were his crowing achievement (Gen. 1:27). It pleased God to make man in his image. Following this, in an effort to exercise their own free will, Adam and Eve disobeyed God; they sought to elevate themselves above him (Gen. 3:5). Because of this, sin has entered into the world and plagued all of creation ever since (Rom. 5:12; 8:22). What is vital to remember is that we are dead in our sins from birth, no longer able to exercise a truly free will because our will is polluted by sin; thus we are in bondage to it (Eph. 2:1; Rom. 3:23; 8:21). Let me extrapolate this issue of free will even further.

When the Reformation spread throughout Europe in the sixteenth century, one of the chief interests at the center of theological discourse was this issue of free will. The problem with many contemporary debates between Calvinists and Arminians is that the issue is *not* whether or not humans have a will and are able to make choices. No one denies this, especially the Calvinist. Undoubtedly, humans can make decisions and those decisions have real consequences. I am free to decide whether or not I want toast or eggs in the morning. If I do not have eggs in the fridge, I am not free to have eggs at that time, unless I am willing to go to the store and get more. But this issue is never whether or not I can decide certain things—that's a given. However, I cannot be a professional hockey player. I am thirty years old and do not have the skills needed to do it. So in this sense, I am not free.

The question is not whether or not we have choices. We do. The issue in the Reformation, as well as the issue between Augustine and Pelagius in the fourth century, was whether or not the will is *free from bondage to sin*. Depending on where you land theologically, you are either free from sin, or not free from sin. I am arguing that you and I are not free from sin and are dead in it, thus in need of a new birth and resurrected heart.

The new birth, or the doctrine of regeneration, is the free act of God alone whereby he renews or resurrects the human heart, taking it from deadness to being alive (see Jn. 3:1-15). When God acts to change a sinner's heart from being dead, he does so freely of his own will and power. He does not look at any goodness (there is none but unrighteousness), but rather extends grace to the sinner. Because all descendants of Adam have inherited a sin nature, we are unable to anything good (Is. 64:6). This does not mean that a not-yet-believer cannot assist an old-lady across the street. It means that he is unable to meet the perfect righteous standard of a holy God, no matter how many good things he tries to do. When Jesus speaks to the religious leader, Nicodemus, he uses the language of being "born again." Jesus says in another passage that, "Apart from me you can do nothing" (Jn. 15:5). The Scripture also says, "Nothing will be impossible with God" (Lk. 1:37). Furthermore, John says, "But to all who did receive him, who believe in his name, he gave the right to become children of God, who were born, not of blood nor the will of the flesh nor of the will of man, but of God (1:12-13).

To quote Jared Wilson:

We are saved from God to God by God through God for God.[3]

In the Old Testament, God promised that *he* would remove the sinner's heart of stone and put in a heart of flesh (Ezek. 36:26). In other words, a heart that has been dead and unmoved will be able to, by the Spirit of God, beat vibrantly with the glory of God. When Jesus speaks of this new birth, this is what he is referring to: God will act out of his own grace via the Holy Spirit to quicken our heart so that we are no longer dead to sin, but alive to righteousness, thus inclining our wills to God (Ezek. 36:27). Once a heart is regenerated, faith is then given to the believer as gift. Stated differently, regeneration precedes faith, and the fruit of regeneration is faith. A heart that is dead in sin cannot exercise faith, but a heart that has been regenerated by God does (Eph. 2:4-10).[4] What is pertinent to remember is that we are not

---

[3] Jared C. Wilson, *Gospel Deeps* (Wheaton, IL: Crossway Books, 2012), 75.

[4] Eph. 2:1-10 is rich in theological content as it pertains to the doctrine of salvation.

talking about good people becoming better or bad people becoming good. We are talking about dead people made alive—language the Bible frequently uses. When we perpetuate the view that it is somehow about good people getting help, we fall into the trap of self-righteousness, something that our hearts love vehemently.

When we speak of salvation, we are not just speaking of immediate deliverance from temporary things, albeit the Old Testament addresses this concept (Ps. 85:8, 9; Is. 62:11). When we talk about Salvation in the capital "S" sense of the word, we are talking about the ultimate vindication of the believer at the Judgment seat of Christ. Salvation delivers the Christian from God's wrath, penalty, power, and presence of sin (Rom. 1:18; 3:9; 5:21; 1 Thess. 5:9). This is the heart of the gospel narrative: that Christ came to die for the ungodly (Rom. 5:6). Salvation is accomplished by what Christ has done on our behalf. We do not accomplish it for ourselves—we cannot. But Christ can accomplish it for us and has irrefutably already done so. Not only has his death defeated Satan, sin and death, he has granted to us, through justification by faith alone, his righteousness (2. Cor. 5:21). He has given us his active obedience through the indwelling power of the Holy Spirit who has taken up residence in us (Jn. 15:4; 17:26; Col. 1:27). Through Salvation, we are united with Christ in his death and resurrection (Rom. 6:3-10; Col. 2:12, 20; 3:1).

At the center of all of this is the doctrine of penal substitutionary atonement. "Penal" refers to the penalty incurred from sin; "substitution" refers to Jesus' death in our place, and "atonement" refers to the ultimate work of Christ's death as it removes God's wrath and expiates our sin. Jesus has stepped in our place; and all of this is so that we can have joy in God (Ps. 16:11).

Amazing.

THE DOCTRINE OF SANCTIFICATION

Paul begins this section by encouraging the Philippian church to obey, not just when Paul is present (for that would be too easy!), but also while he is absent. They are to obey (work out salvation) even while Paul is away.

Do not miss the "therefore" at the beginning of the section. Paul bases this next whole section on the Christ hymn that he has just fleshed out. We are called to be unified as a church, considering others as more important than ourselves. We are to practice and cultivate a humility like Jesus. Jesus is our prime example of humility who obeyed the Father, even to the point of death. And death on the cross at that! Because of his obedience on our behalf, he was exalted to his position of Lord as he rules and reigns over all right now to the glory of God the Father. This is the context of the passage at hand.

Having laid out the doctrine of salvation, I want to go back to this "work" stuff that Paul hones in on.

The Christian life is hard work. It is not as though we muster up the willpower to obey God, and when we do that, we immediately enter into heaven or an idle cruise control of bliss. When we meet Jesus, we do not see an immediate perfection as though we do not need to continue the fight against sin and fight for joy. We unquestionably work, and we work *hard*. The danger, of course, is indifference—something that traps many Christians.

The key, Paul says, is that it is God who does the working *in* us. We work *out* our salvation because God works it *in*. Not only have we been saved, justified, adopted, regenerated and given the presence of the Spirit, we also are granted Christ's righteousness, obedience and *active work inside of us*. This is what Paul intends to convey in this section of Scripture. We do not earn any of this: we are given it by grace through faith. God works in human will (the means) to achieve God's ends (his glory). He does it all for his pleasure. "Our God is in the heavens; he does all that he pleases" (Ps. 115:3).

What's at stake here in this section is the doctrine of sanctification.

The *Westminster Shorter Catechism* defines it for us:

> Sanctification is the work of God's free grace, whereby we are renewed in the whole man after the image of God, and are enabled more and more to die unto sin, and live unto righteousness.[5]

It is the work of God in the life of the believer through the Holy Spirit whereby the gospel is applied in thought, word and deed. The Holy Spirit frees us from the power of sin (perpetually) while granting us new affections for

---

[5] Question 35, *The Westminster Shorter Catechism: With Scripture Proofs*, 3rd edition. (Oak Harbor, WA: Logos Research Systems, Inc., 1996).

Christ. God changes our dispositions, attitudes and outlooks while assisting us in the process of mortifying indwelling sin.

At its root is the word "sanctify," which is to set apart as holy to and for God. The Spirit works to make us look like Jesus (Rom. 8:29). We are not only saved from sin but saved to God and his will and pleasure. Salvation is not an escape from reality; it is participation in the sufferings of Christ (something Paul knew quite well) as God works in us for his mission. If regeneration is the new birth, then sanctification is new growth. When God puts himself inside of us, he gives us new delights, treasures and joys. We love the things we used to hate, and now hate the things we used to love. He gives us a desire to give him glory, growing in holiness through the reading of God's word and prayer. God does not only give us new desires—he helps us accomplish them, too (Phil. 2:12-13).

Furthermore, while regeneration and justification are one-time declarations of God on behalf of the sinner, sanctification is an ongoing process of dependence on God as we fight against sin and fight for joy. Since we are unable to meet the perfect standard of God's holiness and righteousness, he does it for us in Christ as it is applied to the believer through the Holy Spirit. The Trinity is involved in the process from start to finish.

When it is all said and done, there is a war within the believer (Rom. 7:14-25). The flesh wishes to gratify itself with sin while the regenerating work of the Spirit wishes to fight sin and find greater satisfaction in God. Remember, this is work. It takes the constant renewal of the mind and the constant fight against sin and temptation. We should never place our faith and fight for holiness in neutral; we must pursue it, for God is at work within us. Thomas Watson is helpful yet again:

> Salvation must not only be sought out by knowledge, but wrought out by practice: "Work out your own salvation with fear and trembling." There can be no crown without running; no reward without diligence.[6]

What is fascinating about Paul's admonition here is that we are to do all of this with "fear and trembling." Translated another way, we are to do this with "awe and reverence." We are to work at this salvation, persevering as God preserves us. This does not mean that we have an anxiety towards the unknown but that we respect the known. As God works inside of us through the Spirit, he draws us back to the holiness of God and in doing so, we can only respond with reverence and gratitude for the gospel. Neither do this mean that we question our salvation as though God cannot competently save a sinner. It means that we are his, and he is good. Again, no one can boast next to the cross, and Paul's point is fixed on humility as the passage before has clearly laid out. "Serve the Lord with fear, and rejoice with trembling" (Ps. 2:11).

---

[6] Thomas Watson, *Puritan Gems*, ed. John Adey (London: J. Snow and Ward, 1850), 118.

LIVING IN THE WORLD

In Phil. 2:6-11, Paul gives us the pattern and example of Christ. When Paul uses Jesus as an example, he does not mean to use him as an example in the sense of an abstract concept, but instead has at the heart of his theology a vision of our union with Christ.[7] As the last chapter noted, our humility is the fruit of Jesus' righteousness and obedience, not something that is in the natural self (for pride is the fruit of sin). Coming out of this passage, then, is the command to work out the salvation that God has worked in us because God is at work. Paul then moves to how we are to function as individuals in community:

> Do all things without grumbling or disputing, that you may be blameless and innocent, children of God without blemish in the midst of a crooked and twisted generation, among whom you shine as lights in the world, holding fast to the word of life, so that in the day of Christ I may be proud that I did not run in vain or labor in vain. Even if I am to be poured out as a drink offering upon the sacrificial offering of your faith, I am glad and rejoice with you all. Likewise you also should be glad and rejoice with me.[8]

As I have mentioned before, there is never a command

---

[7] For a concise look at this concept of union with Christ, see Kevin DeYoung, *The Hole in Our Holiness* (Wheaton, IL: Crossway Books, 2012), 93-105.

[8] Phil. 2:14-18.

in Scripture given without a truth underneath it. When Paul says to "do all things…" he says to do them within the context of the aforementioned things, namely, the example of Christ's humility and the fact that God is at work in us. God is oftentimes more interested in the person than the work itself. In other words, the command is for the believer to do something altogether countercultural from the world and never just for the outcome—God wants to work and grow the believer.

If we start with the command with no context of truth behind it, we fall into the trap of self-righteousness—something Jesus condemns over and over again.[9] In contrast, for us to accomplish what Paul has in mind we must always go back to the gospel.

Verses 14-15 are an echo from a passage in the Old Testament. In Deuteronomy 32, Moses gives a charge to the Israelites before they enter the promised land. (Moses knew at this point that he was not going to be allowed to go into it.) He gives this same exact charge as a dying man preaching to dying men. He, like Paul was running out of time, and needed to convey some last minute information that would hopefully lead to transformation. Moses reminds the Israelites of whom God is and what God has done and how they are to live in light of that knowledge. Paul sees himself as Moses.

Paul's exhortation is not for us to be like the world that values self over all. The Philippians are not to be like the whiny, oftentimes incessantly complaining

---

[9] See, for example, Matthew 23:1-36.

people in the world who are never content. Rather, they are to do all things as God would have them to do. As God works in our wills for his glory, they are never to grumble or dispute so that they can be blameless (see Phil. 1:10). This grumbling and disputing echoes back to the story of the Israelites and their perpetual complaints coming out of Egypt. Paul sees the work of Jesus as a New Exodus, one that is unleashed upon the world through the King's good news. He also believes that they are to function as the true children of God in such a way as to stand out in society as "lights."[10]

How are we to live as lights?

To start, we must acknowledge the darkness of the world. "I have come into the world a light," Jesus said, "so that whoever believes in me may not remain in darkness" (Jn. 12:46). The light of the world has come and brought with him salvation.

In Daniel 12:3 we read: "And those who are wise shall shine like brightness of the sky above; and those who turn many to righteousness, like the stars forever and ever." Paul is echoing Daniel who spoke about the "wise," those Israelites who followed the law, and "those who turn many to righteousness," being the same. These Israelites would shine brightly in a world of darkness as they pursued the living God in the midst of suffering. Not only that, the passage is connected with the promise that God would raise the dead (Dan. 12:2). The Israelites, along with the Philippian church, were to be signs of life

---

[10] Take note that Israel was called to be a light to the nations. See Is. 42:6.

in a world of darkness.

At the center of this is the "word of life," the gospel, that we are to cling to which is in direct contradiction to the promise of sin that leads to death. Paul is a man of eschatological fervor. He understands death and what life truly means (Phil. 1:21). He also knows that the day of Messiah will come when the entire world will be put to rights. He does not wish to be disappointed with his beloved church. This is why he refers to the drink offering found in Numbers 15.[11] He knows that the Philippian church is going to be a sacrifice for the gospel, as they have already shown, and his potential date with death will simply be "icing on the cake" so to speak. Both he and his church are united in an inseparable bond—a bond that even death itself cannot break. This is the reason Paul can rejoice amidst his suffering. He sees a greater event on the horizon, one that includes the appearance of Jesus to restore all things. Like an artist who steps back to take a birds-eye-view of his artwork, Paul wishes to look at his work in appreciation, knowing that he has done all he can do to fulfill God's calling in his life of planting churches so that God will get glory; this is all the more reason for the church to rejoice with Paul.

---

[11] The drink offering (libation) was symbolic of the firstfruits of the laborer. Drinking wine was connected to victory and Sabbath rest. Wine was also poured on top of an animal sacrifice and then the wine went up in smoke. Paul's work is lifted up as a special drink to God to make God's heart glad. This is how Paul sees the New Covenant working out: suffering for and with and in Messiah.

WITH OTHERS

Paul moves out of these commands to showcase two exemplary men, connecting his exhortation to practical examples of godliness in the midst of a crooked generation. First is Timothy:

> I hope in the Lord Jesus to send Timothy to you soon, so that I too may be cheered by news of you. For I have no one like him, who will be genuinely concerned for your welfare. For they all seek their own interests, not those of Jesus Christ. But you know Timothy's proven worth, how as a son with a father he has served with me in the gospel. I hope therefore to send him just as soon as I see how it will go with me, and I trust in the Lord that shortly I myself will come also.[12]

Paul has a strong history with young Timothy. He met him on his first missionary journey and spent a lot of time training him (Acts 16:1-5). Though a timid young pastor, Paul takes this opportunity to send a quick letter of reference to the Philippian church so that they are encouraged by Timothy's coming Paul also wants to keep the church informed about how he is doing.

This brief portrait of Timothy can give us some food for thought regarding how we are to be in the world, with others. Paul does not begin this section by peddling Timothy and his astounding preaching capabilities. He does not say that Timothy is a super-Christian with a dose of extra holiness. Paul says that Timothy will be

---

[12] Phil. 2:19-24.

genuinely concerned about the welfare of the church. In other words, Timothy will serve them with humility, a true mark of service.

For Paul, this is the true mark of a shepherd-pastor. A pastor is one who cares for his sheep. In a day and age where pastors act like rock stars, comedians and artists, Paul seems to say that true pastors care for their sheep above all else. Apparently Paul sees the interests of Christ Jesus as being the same as being concerned with others, and indeed they are! Timothy has labored alongside Paul in the gospel, by planting churches and releasing them out to make disciples of all nations. Serving Jesus is the same as serving the church because the two are inseparable.

The exact thing Paul has laid out in verses 1-4 (see the last chapter) is the exact thing that Timothy has done. Timothy has learned to put the concerns of others ahead of his own. Rather than touting his seminary degree and ability to parse Greek verbs, Paul hold up Timothy as an example of what it means to be in the world, with others. In sending Timothy to the church, Paul sees his network expand—and an expansive network of local churches it was. Timothy understands the gospel, and the gospel is not mere facts about Jesus: it is putting the needs of others before your own (see Mt. 22:36-40).

Having set up Timothy as a gospel example, Paul closes out the chapter by speaking of Epaphroditus (which means, "charming"):

> I have thought it necessary to send to you Epaphroditus
> my brother and fellow worker and fellow soldier, and
> your messenger and minister to my need, for he has
> been longing for you all and has been distressed because
> you heard that he was ill. Indeed he was ill, near to
> death. But God had mercy on him, and not only on him
> but on me also, lest I should have sorrow upon sorrow. I
> am the more eager to send him, therefore, that you may
> rejoice at seeing him again, and that I may be less
> anxious. So receive him in the Lord with all joy, and
> honor such men, for he nearly died for the work of
> Christ, risking his life to complete what was lacking in
> your service to me.[13]

Epaphroditus made the 800-mile trip (in probably 6-weeks) from Philippi to Rome to see Paul and bring him assistance. In doing so, Epaphroditus literally risked his life, traveling through horrendous conditions, coming to fulfill the service that was lacking (the service they had not been able to perform or complete). Paul says that he is a brother (true family), a fellow worker (a laborer in the gospel), a soldier (fighting for joy), a messenger (keeping in touch with Paul as a representative from Philippi) and minister (serving Paul and others).

Apparently Epaphroditus nearly died. From what, we do not know, but God has mercy on him and Paul wishes to send him back to the church so that the gospel can continue to go forward.

What is unique about these two examples is that we

---

[13] Phil. 2:25-30.

get behind the mind and emotions of Paul. These two passages are not just about those two godly men—they are about Paul and his wrestling with sorrow and joy. Paul says that he nearly had sorrow upon sorrow, and we could criticize Paul for not fighting for joy, but we would be wrong. He is fighting for joy. But emotions are real for Paul. These are his friends and family, and he loves them genuinely. When I say that we are to fight for joy, I am *not* saying that you should set aside your feelings, and neither is Paul. We are constantly called to revisit the gospel and be reminded of what is at stake in life. Being in the world, with others, requires us to fight to believe in a future grace that will sustain us. Grace does not come to us in Jesus alone; it comes to us through him, coupled with hope.

FINAL THOUGHTS

At our church, we are seeing gospel communities on mission spring up. Missional communities are pockets and groups of people who gather each week as an expression of the gospel. Mere Sunday programs cannot make disciples. There has to be a context in which disciples are built. If we are to be in the world with others, we must be able to do life through the thick and thin. The beauty behind this section of Scripture is the unity found in the example of Paul and the Philippian church. Remember that Paul was facing death and at any moment could be sentenced to it. Paul is fighting for joy and he does it *with others*. The individual pursuit of joy and holiness is indispensable, but it cannot be separated from the body of Christ, for the body of Christ is the visible expression of Jesus in the world.

Sanctification is the continual awakening of our gospel identity. Our identity is discovered in the Trinity: the Father has made us family; the Son has made us servants; and the Spirit has shaped us as a community of missionaries. What jumps off the page in this section of Philippians is the fact that being in the world as a church with others matters. These are not meager concepts here. They are real and raw, and we would do well to listen carefully.

Where has the church missed her identity?

Not only this, but, since Jesus has done what he has done, how now shall we live?

JASON M. GARWOOD

7 - WITH CHRIST'S RIGHTEOUSNESS

Finally, my brothers, rejoice in the Lord. To write the same things to you is no trouble to me and is safe for you. Look out for the dogs, look out for the evildoers, look out for those who mutilate the flesh. For we are the circumcision, who worship by the Spirit of God and glory in Christ Jesus and put no confidence in the flesh—though I myself have reason for confidence in the flesh also. If anyone else thinks he has reason for confidence in the flesh, I have more: circumcised on the eighth day, of the people of Israel, of the tribe of Benjamin, a Hebrew of Hebrews; as to the law, a Pharisee; as to zeal, a persecutor of the church; as to righteousness under the law, blameless. But whatever gain I had, I counted as loss for the sake of Christ. Indeed, I count everything as loss because of the surpassing worth of knowing Christ Jesus my Lord. For his sake I have suffered the loss of all things and count them as rubbish, in order that I may gain Christ and be found in him, not having a righteousness of my own that comes from the law, but that which comes through faith in Christ, the righteousness from God that depends on faith—that I may know him and the power of his resurrection, and may share his sufferings, becoming like him in his death, that by any means possible I may attain the resurrection from the dead.[1]

Whathat people in the church need to hear more today than anything else is doctrinal teaching. And not the ordinary theological lecture as we might suppose, but rather the theological exaltation of God that reveals the depths of the wisdom of God. We do not need the moralistic therapy that comes from the lips of many preachers, seeking to help you "cope" with the "mistakes and issues" of your life. "Just stay positive," the preacher says, "You'll be fine. Just take it easy and do better next time." This is not the gospel, and this is not helpful. There has to be more than just sin management and sin minimization. You need a savior—an obedient savior no less—one who can stand in your place on your behalf.

If we honestly think about it, we are all guilty of saying these types of things. In fact, several of us are guilty each and every year as we "turn over a new leaf" after the holidays and make a promise to ourselves that we will get more exercise and eat right. We vow to do better, think better thoughts, and try hard not to say something disrespectful to someone. None of these are necessarily evil, but they are not enough. Behavior modification has changed no one's heart.

As a pastor, I counsel with many different people. More often than not, the central issue that I end up

---

[1] Phil. 3:1-11.

getting back to is the heart and its role for the person (Pr. 4:23). For example, in marriage counseling scenarios, not only do I hear a lot of complaints about the other person (and no ownership of their own sins!), I also find that many problems end up being an issue of gender role confusion and the heart's response. The man is not leading as he ought, and the woman is trying to take his leadership role. The origin of this discussion is the issue of the heart: you have issues in your marriage, or whatever circumstance you find yourself in, and instead of examining your own heart, you point the finger. If I tell this couple just to think better thoughts about themselves and each other, and never get around to the gospel and their subsequent identity. Suddenly, behavior modification is all they have to work on, and they will never get anywhere because their hearts are the problem, not just their behavior. To illustrate, this is like a person who wants to kill the weeds in their yard by using scissors to cut off the very top, rather than ripping it out by its roots. Said another way, it's like putting a Band-Aid on a shotgun wound—it is not sufficient.

Looking back on my pastoral ministry thus far, I have become convinced of one thing with absolute certainty: more gospel has never hurt anyone. This reinforces my initial argument: more doctrine (teaching) leads to more doxology (praise of God). If we rely on the Holy Spirit and revel in the plethora of treasures we find in the gospel, we will change because our hearts will change. What is required is a deeper knowledge of the Scriptures and a stronger comprehension of our new found identities.

My hope in this chapter is for us to grab hold of more doctrine, not so we can puff ourselves up, but so we can hold more tightly to God himself and marvel at how marvelous he is. The study of doctrine is intended to send you into God-glorifying moments of worship as you reflect on whom he is and what he has done for you in Christ. That is its purpose.

THE MORALISTIC BALANCING ACT

Before I dive into the text, I want to address the moralistic balancing act that many Christians have fell into regarding how a person (1) gets saved and (2) grows in sanctification.

To begin, all of us have an inner lawyer that screams for justice. Whether it is defending our case or prosecuting someone else—we love justice. We love to enact it, and we love to vindicate ourselves with it.

For example, take the married couple I alluded to earlier. If a husband is lazy at home and does not help with the housework or kids, then the wife who stays at home all day with them may feel unappreciated. "I work for a living so I can come home and not work. Besides, this is your job," says the husband. Indeed the stay-at-home mom is to make a home, but the issue is not job titles and job duties. The issue is service. Are you as a husband going to serve your wife as you are called to do?

"You never help around the house. You never tell me that you love me," says the wife, and justifiably so. The husband, who activates his justice radar and inner lawyer, retorts, "I do tell you that I love you and I mowed the grass and just painted the fence to prove it!"

Do you see what is happening? Justice is happening. Instead of owning up to his faults, he tries to vindicate his case and throw it back on his spouse. Instead of repenting from his sins and shortcomings, he declares himself in the right (just/righteous) and proceeds to retaliate or exert more justice on his wife. The circle of justice is in full swing in this home.

Whether you admit it or not, sin distorts our perception of justice. I call this the "moralistic balancing act" because a balancing act is what we do as believers who are following Jesus. This can show its ugly head in several different ways. Sometimes it shows as we learn to deal with our conscience that accuses us; it also happens when we feel the weight of the law of God that brings us under judgment.

For example, think for a moment about the last time someone confronted you. How did you respond? Were you upset? Did you get defensive? Did you listen to the person intently, trying to understand where he/she is coming from? How we deal with confrontation, is just one of several of the ways we balance justice in our lives. If something is wrong with us and we know it, we would do well to take ownership of this problem and repent of it instead of trying to vindicate ourselves and respond back as a prosecuting attorney.

When it comes to salvation, many folks believe that their good works will earn them heaven. Because of the indifference and apathy of many evangelicals, a lot of people do not even think this anymore. Many are not worried whether or not their good works will get them into heaven; no, most believe that what they are doing right now will suffice. As if God loves indifference to his glory. As if God would let a lukewarm nobody into his presence. His holiness is never compromised.

We shall come back to this issue of works after laying the groundwork from the Old Testament.

ISRAEL, COVENANT, AND JUSTIFICATION

This entire chapter revolves around the story of redemption and how a holy God has achieved the impossible task of restoring sinful man to himself. While Jesus is certainly the apex of the story of redemption, it all starts in Genesis.

If you recall, our first parents, Adam and Eve, broke the covenant of works by eating of the tree that they were forbidden to partake of. Because of this, God made an animal sacrifice to appease his justice and cover their guilt (Gen. 3:21). When the two realized they were naked, the feeling of shame kicked in for the first time, and the two were marked as transgressors of God's law. Here is an exciting act of redemption, second, I suppose, only to God's decision to create. God stepped in and provided for what the sinners could not provide for themselves.

As the story goes on, Genesis 12 rolls around and a man named Abram receives a calling to "go." Again, God refuses to leave his sin-trodden creation to go to waste. Instead, he enters in and forms another covenant, this time with Abraham. In Genesis 15:1-6 God says something profound to Abraham:

After these things the word of the LORD came to Abram in a vision: "Fear not, Abram, I am your shield; your reward shall be very great." But Abram said, "O Lord GOD, what will you give me, for I continue childless, and the heir of my house is Eliezer of Damascus?" And Abram said, "Behold, you have given me no offspring, and a member of my household will be my heir." And behold, the word of the LORD came to him: "This man shall not be your heir; your very own son shall be your heir." And he brought him outside and said, "Look toward heaven, and number the stars, if you are able to number them." Then he said to him, "So shall your offspring be." And he believed the LORD, and he counted it to him as righteousness.

The last phrase, "And he counted it to him as righteousness," is what ought to be mind blowing. Here is Abram. He is a foreigner in a strange land. He used to be a pagan. However, God uses him to begin his new creation project in the form of a Jewish nation. This happens before he is given the son of the promise. Before Abram can do anything righteous, God counts him as righteous simply because Abram *believed*.

Let me explain to you what I mean by "righteousness." In short, righteousness is covenant faithfulness to the law of God. Without a doubt, and this will be beneficial to remember in the next section, God's law must be fulfilled perfectly if someone is going to go to heaven. You *must* perform works and be perfect (Mt. 5:48). In sum: to be righteous is to fulfill the law of God in some manner and be deemed "in the right" (just) in the eyes of God as a faithful covenant keeper.

As the story progresses, the Israelites are redeemed from slavery in Egypt under the leadership of Moses. In Exodus 19, the Israelites arrive at Mount Sinai. It is here that God promises to Israel that she will be his treasured possession if she keep his commandments (Ex. 19:5-6). Following this, in chapter 20, Israel is given the Ten Commandments. As the story progresses yet again, we arrive at Deuteronomy 29 when the covenant is renewed at Moab, just before Israel enters the promised land. If Israel does well and obeys, things will go good for them. If they fail, they will not be in the land terribly long (30:19).

After entering the land, Israel's sin accumulates and it does not take long for things to go bad. In 722 B.C., Assyria destroys the Northern Kingdom, several hundred years after the time of King David (circa 1000 B.C.). One hundred and thirty-six years later, Babylon comes and destroys Jerusalem and hauls the Jewish people in the Southern Kingdom off to the foreign land. All of this because of their sinful whoredom (see Hos. 1:2).

Throughout the Old Testament, God sends his prophets to woo Israel back to the covenant, but to no avail. Israel is unwilling to repent and because of this, many of the prophets are killed. Over and over again, God sends his messengers, yet no one will listen. The covenant was grossly violated, and yet no one is willing to repent.

Herein lies the perpetual problem in the Old Testament, and I will leave Job's words for you to ponder:

How can a man be in the right before God?[2]

The perennial question in the Old Testament, as well as the New—from Genesis to Revelation—is this question: "Where is your righteousness?" How can someone who is a perpetual covenant breaker ever stand before the only perfect covenant keeper and be declared "in the right"? Said another way: how can a sinner stand in front of a holy and righteous God and be not only absolved from sin, but given a right standing in the court?

This is *the* question.

Have you asked it? Have you ever thought about it? What would be your answer?

When the Old Testament closes out, it does so on a note of uncertainty. There are questions that the Jewish people have. They are in exile, and they want to know when a New Exodus is going to come. The land of promise is rightfully still theirs, but they are not living there.

Where is the righteous Israelite who will lead the way?

Has God abandoned his covenant people?

Is God truly just if we are still in exile?

These are the questions, and they are hard ones indeed.

---

[2] Job 9:2.

JESUS AND THE JUSTIFICATION OF GOD

One of the challenges for the modern reader and average church-goer as I see it, is that people do not often see the ongoing connection between the Old Testament and the New. Aside from a few typological guesses, what I have just outlined in the previous section may come as something new to you. Rest assure this is not new. The overwhelming problem in the Old Testament is this issue of God's righteousness (Ps. 98:1-3; 143:1). Yes, the Jews understood that they had maligned the covenant. They got that part. But where is God to step in and help them? When is he going to come to their rescue as he did in the days of Moses and David? When are they going to be vindicated? You must deal with this tension before you can understand all that Jesus says and does.

What the New Testament affirms loud and clear is that God is, in fact, just and that Jesus is the righteous Israelite that they have been waiting for. Paul says in Romans 1:16-17 that God's righteousness (his covenant keeping faithfulness) has been revealed in the gospel, namely, in the person and work of Jesus. What Jesus does in his ministry and sacrificial death, and subsequent resurrection, is vindicate God as just. At the same time, God affirms Christ's death as sufficient while vindicating Jesus, too (1 Tim. 3:16). In other words, the problem left in the Old Testament has now reached its solution.

When Jesus ascends back to the Father to inherit his throne in Acts 1, there is a new problem that arises: now what are the disciples to do? They thought the kingdom was now going to be restored to Israel (Acts 1:6), but instead Jesus instructs them to go and wait until the Spirit comes. As the story unfolds the church expands through the preaching of the gospel. Not only do many Jews respond, Gentiles begin to respond through the ministry of Peter, too (see Acts 10). As Gentiles begin to repentant and trust in Jesus as Lord, a new problem arises in the early church. How does one become a part of God's new covenant family? Acts 15 happens next, and the Jerusalem Council affirms that Gentiles do *not* first have to become Jewish in order to become Christians. Gentiles do not have to be circumcised, nor do they have to observe the traditional Jewish laws of ceremony and ritual.

Through it all, Jesus' perfectly obedient life, death, resurrection, ascension and sending of the church breaks down all racial, gender and socio-economic barriers (Gal. 3:28). How can you become part of God's new covenant family? By faith, just like Abraham's story. Is God righteous and faithful? Yes.

THE TEXT
Paul opens us this next section with a bold proclamation:

> Finally, my brothers, rejoice in the Lord. To write the same things to you is no trouble to me and is safe for you. Look out for the dogs, look out for the evildoers, look out for those who mutilate the flesh. For we are the circumcision, who worship by the Spirit of God and glory in Christ Jesus and put no confidence in the

flesh—[3]

Paul is comfortable writing to the church because of their relationship and it is "safe" to address something of utter importance, namely that there is a gospel, and we ought to not mess with it.

In accordance to Jewish law, a male was to be circumcised on the eighth day (Gen. 17:1-14). In doing so, the perpetual covenant that God made with Abraham progressed along as the Jewish people were marked out in the world for God and his purposes.

What Paul is addressing here he frames within the larger context of his theology elsewhere. You will need to read Galatians and Romans to get a larger picture of the concern that Paul has with those who say one must become Jewish in order to become Christian (they are called the "Judaizers").

What Paul affirms here for the Philippian church is that the real "dogs" are the ones who are propagating the idea that you cannot be a follower of Jesus unless you are circumcised and observe other Jewish laws. Normally the Jews would call Gentile people dogs (not a common house pet at this time!), but Paul switches the term and ferociously accuses them of being the actual "dogs." He says that they are the ones who mutilate their flesh thinking it does something to earn them a status! "In [Christ] also you were circumcised with a circumcision made without hands, by putting off the

---

[3] Phil. 3:1-3.

body of the flesh, by the circumcision of Christ" (Col. 2:11).

What is key to understanding Paul's theology is the connection between the Spirit's new work in the heart verses the law's work in the flesh:

> For circumcision indeed is of value if you obey the law, but if you break the law, your circumcision becomes uncircumcision. So, if a man who is uncircumcised keeps the precepts of the law, will not is uncircumcision be regarded as circumcision? Then he who is physically uncircumcised but keeps the law will condemn you who have the written code and circumcision but break the law. For no one is a Jew who is merely one outwardly, nor is circumcision outward and physical. But a Jew is one inwardly, and circumcision is a matter of the heart, by the Spirit, not by the letter.[4]

As Gentiles come into the New Covenant, these Jewish laws become the center of discussion. As these verses in Romans illustrate, circumcision came *after* Abraham was credited righteousness (Rom. 4:11); therefore, the argument is null and void because righteousness cannot come from the law. Knowledge of sin comes from the law (Rom. 3:19-20). Our trespasses increase because of the law, too (Rom. 5:20). Being found guilty of unrighteousness, Paul says, there cannot be a righteousness attainable through the law no matter how

---

[4] Rom. 2:25-29.

good and perfect it is. Circumcision is a matter of the heart. Our hearts are what needs to be changed (Jer. 17:9).

How does one worship God, then, if fleshly matters are not what is essential? Paul says that the truly "circumcised" (in the heart) worship by the Spirit of God and give weight and centrality to Jesus, putting zero confidence in the flesh. Jesus takes centrality, not the foreskin or Jewishness.

Paul continues:

> Though I myself have reason for confidence in the flesh also. If anyone else thinks he has reason for confidence in the flesh, I have more: circumcised on the eighth day, of the people of Israel, of the tribe of Benjamin, a Hebrew of Hebrews; as to the law, a Pharisee; as to zeal, a persecutor of the church; as to righteousness under the law, blameless.[5]

At the heart of Paul's argument you will find his résumé and credentials that speak loud and clear of his achievements and personal righteousness.

Paul has more reason to have confidence in his Jewish heritage and self-performance (flesh) than most people. He was circumcised on the eighth day, and not later like many had done. He was a full-blooded Jew, one who descended from the great tribe of Benjamin (the only clan that stuck with Judah after the split in the kingdom). He was a "Hebrew of Hebrews," and in

---

[5] Phil. 3:4-6.

relation to the law, he was a Pharisee, which meant he taught the law and would have had it memorized. In terms of his passion and zeal of defending Judaism, he tried to smite the early followers of Jesus. With regard to his covenant faithfulness, he was blameless (not perfect, but close!). Paul had it all. If anyone could consider their flesh[6] as being top notch, it was Paul. He had gain.

But...

> But whatever gain I had, I counted as loss for the sake of Christ. Indeed, I count everything as loss because of the surpassing worth of knowing Christ Jesus my Lord. For his sake I have suffered the loss of all things and count them as rubbish, in order that I may gain Christ and be found in him, not having a righteousness of my own that comes from the law, but that which comes through faith in Christ, the righteousness from God that depends on faith—that I may know him and the power of his resurrection, and may share his sufferings, becoming like him in his death, that by any means possible I may attain the resurrection from the dead.[7]

Paul saw that all of the "gain" he had in the credit side of his account must be considered a "loss" because of Christ's surpassing worth. Because Christ is supreme and of ultimate value, anything else is refuse. Paul does not just know Christ (like how we know what the color blue

---

[6] Again, read "flesh" to mean "heritage," or "Jewishness," as well as the old nature and sinfully depraved body we are born with.

[7] Phil. 3:7-11.

looks like), he *knows* him to the point of suffering with and for him. He even considers the most righteous and "good" things that he has as loss so that he can be found in Messiah, having a righteousness that is outside of his own moral effort and given to him as a gift in the person and work of Jesus. How does Paul get this righteousness? By faith.

This passage, along with portions of Romans and Galatians, is ground zero for the doctrine of justification. As touched on back in chapter 2, justification is central to the gospel. Without this doctrine, the whole of the gospel collapses into oblivion. Let me explain this a bit more as a reminder that fighting for joy with Christ's righteousness is a fight to believe and treasure our justification.

Before the heavenly courtroom, God declares the Christian righteous by grace alone, through faith alone, in Christ alone. Though Adam sinned and all died in him, Christ obeyed and many were made righteous (Rom. 5:18-19). Our salvation and justification is granted, not by the intensity of our faith, but on the objectivity of Jesus. When God declares us righteous, he does it because of what Jesus has done, not by what we have done. Our works, no matter how good or bad, cannot be used. Many believe that there are various gradations of human righteousness, but the Bible shuts this down fairly quickly: we are sinful and he is holy. Because of this, God must declare us "in the right," for we cannot do so on our own.

To God be the glory!

God has sent Christ, accepted his work as sufficient,

imputes (reckons/credits) his work to our account, gives us the will and faith to believe, and does it all for his glory. This is our God! Even the faith to believe is a gift (Eph. 2:8-9). Justification is an act of grace, so much so that even the means by which we are justified (faith) is a gift from God. God produces in us the will and act of believing.

What is crucial to understand here is that when God looks at the believer, he sees her as if she always obeyed, and as if she had never sinned. God does *not* see a fallen sinner, but a redeemed sinner. Theologically, the Christian is *simul justus et peccator* (at the same time just/righteous and sinner). Our old sinful nature has been crucified with Christ (Gal. 2:20), however, we still carry around this body of death (Rom. 7:24) and need to beat it up from time-to-time (1 Cor. 9:27). The issue is *not* what good works we can offer up, but rather what good work Christ has done on our behalf. I mentioned beforehand that God imputes the righteousness of Jesus to the believer. The doctrine of justification is secure in this concept: God takes our sin and lays it upon Christ, and then takes Christ's righteousness and credits it to our account (2 Cor. 5:21). This is God at work from start to finish!

I want to take a moment and address this issue as it pertains to Roman Catholic theology and Reformed theology. Oftentimes people assume that Roman Catholic theology teaches that one is saved by good works. This is only partially true. The Roman Catholic formula for justification is that faith and works equals justification. The biblical formula is that faith equals justification and works. While the Reformed view teaches imputation, the Roman Catholic view teaches infusion. No one argues that God alone justifies. The issue is *on what grounds.* In Roman Catholic theology, you must do sacraments and spark some sort of righteousness inside of yourself in order for God to then infuse his righteousness. Be careful though, otherwise it will be removed if you commit a mortal sin. This is called the *analytical* view of justification. What the Bible teaches, as well as Reformed theology, is a *synthetic* view of justification. We are dead in our sins, and God credits (reckons/imputes) Christ's righteousness to us, and it is never withdrawn. We did not do anything good or bad to earn it; therefore, we cannot do anything good or bad to keep it. It is ours *in Christ.* The Roman Catholic must cooperate with God in order to get this justification and even if he gets it, there is never a guarantee it will always be there.

THE FIGHT FOR JOY WITH CHRIST'S RIGHTEOUSNESS

Quite frankly, the Roman Catholic view is *not* the gospel. It is far from the gospel of grace. For the Roman Catholic Church, faith is necessary for justification, but it is not sufficient. You must try a little harder to help God along in his justification project. Be warned: *even your good works still qualify for repentance.*

If we think for a moment that we can contribute anything to our salvation and justification, then we are mocking God and belittling his grace.

Part of fighting for joy is believing that true joy is knowing Jesus. Happiness is circumstantial, but joy is unwavering because joy is based upon the rock solid objectivity of Jesus. The heart of Paul's thinking in this passage is that Christ is enough. He is more than adequate. He is so sufficient that nothing else we do, no matter how noble, good and righteous. Nothing else will give us the deep and abiding joy that only comes from Christ. Paul sees all of his credentials as rubbish (literally "dung"), so that he can be justified (vs. 9), sanctified (vs. 10), and glorified (vs. 11). All of this is worth more than anything because it is of supreme worth and will never fade.

Joy can be had because God gives to us Christ's righteousness. Stop trying to prove yourself to God and other people. The work is done. You're not impressive, but Christ is impressive. You can prop yourself up to look morally acceptable, or you can fight for joy knowing that Christ's righteousness is sufficient! That is the difference between fighting for an abiding joy in Christ with what he gives us, and fighting for an elusive joy in Christ that is ultimately about us because we think we are something and have something to offer. Truth be told, it gets exhausting.

JASON M. GARWOOD

8 - WHEN YOU ARE TIRED

Not that I have already obtained this or am already perfect, but I press on to make it my own, because Christ Jesus has made me his own. Brothers, I do not consider that I have made it my own. But one thing I do: forgetting what lies behind and straining forward to what lies ahead, I press on toward the goal for the prize of the upward call of God in Christ Jesus. Let those of us who are mature think this way, and if in anything you think otherwise, God will reveal that also to you. Only let us hold true to what we have attained.[1]

I get it, I honestly do. I understand the impulse to want to prove yourself. I understand the drive within myself to want to make "me" look good so that people will notice. We all do it. We love to be looked upon as valued and prized. We want to be wanted and need to be needed. Whether we think we need validation from others to prove we have worth, or

---
[1] Phil. 3:12-16.

whether we need to control things, the human nature bent on sin makes an idol out of feeling esteemed by things that are not God. Indeed, to be esteemed by someone you esteem is of massive significance. However, for many of us, we look to things horizontally (instead of vertically towards God) to fulfill this need. Be it relationships, social media or technology—we all have the inner drive to grab glory for ourselves. This shows up in various ways, of course. We tend to have a hard time dealing with criticism and failure. Oftentimes we find it hard to relax in a world that is constantly moving. If someone succeeds ahead of us, we become proud and envious of that person. Finally, it shows up when we tend to react towards people in such a way as to make them feel guilty. All of these are signs that point to the reality that we enjoy being in the spotlight. We thrive on it. We fight for it. We embrace it without reservation.

Truth be told: *it's exhausting.*

While I've never heard nor read of anyone ever suggesting what I'm about to say, I think it is astonishingly true and significant: sin is tiring. The reason it is tiring is because it is *not* God-centered (who promises to be of help and ease[2]) and if our joy is not rooted in the source of infinite joy, then it will be given to things of finite value and in the end they will prove to be unable to be satisfied. We will constantly be feeding our idols with energy we do not have, and the only

---

[2] "Take my yoke upon you, and learn from me, for I am gentle and lowly in heart, and you will find rest for your souls. For my yoke is easy, and my burden is light" (Mt. 11:29-30).

logical outcome is exhaustion. Idols are never satisfied.

And surely that is at the heart of sin. It is a fight for joy in things that are not God; things that claim to be God but are never able to live up to their calling because we give them a deficient god-like status.

The assertion I just sketched out is a perfect example. If we think for a moment that our being esteemed by others is of ultimate importance, we are, in that moment, substituting God for ourselves. We are saying that since God does not satisfy us enough, we must get validation elsewhere. Without a doubt, it is a question of identity. We are identity thieves. Instead of our being esteemed coming from our new-found identity in Christ, we look for it elsewhere. But God is good, so we don't have to look elsewhere for satisfaction because Jesus is the Father's gift to us and he is *more than* enough.

DOCTRINAL CONTEXT

In the previous two chapters, I sketched some pretty intense doctrinal matters for us because it is exceptionally weighty and has everything to do with this chapter and section of Philippians. As I have asserted before, doctrine leads to doxology, and if it doesn't, then it's not doctrine, but idol worship. What I mean is if we study God to know more information so that we can tout it and flaunt it in front of others, we have officially taken the truths about God and made it an idol, which is the exact opposite of what it is intended to do. (Still don't believe in Total Depravity?)

What's at stake here in the fight for joy when you are tired is embedded in these doctrinal matters. To recap:

Salvation from start to finish is God's work. He changes the dead sinner's heart from a heart of stone to a heart of flesh that beats for his glory. Man contributes nothing but his dead unable-to-be-made-alive-in-and-of-itself-carcass, to salvation. Our good works and performance cannot in any way earn us salvation. Yes, we are saved by works. God's law must be fulfilled, and we must be perfect. The reason we need Jesus' righteousness is because we need his works, not ours. His active and passive obedience is credited to us because we cannot fulfill the law as he did. Soli Deo Gloria!

The same is true for sanctification. We cannot grow in our walk with God and the pursuit of holiness by *mere* moral effort. It is God who works in us (Phil. 2:13) and changes our will to honor him. We cannot, in our sanctification, earn God's favor or somehow get more of it; it is all ours in Christ. It is the Spirit of God who cultivates in us a passion for Jesus. This is gospel-centrality on the ground.

Not only did we talk at length about salvation and sanctification, we talked in the last chapter about justification. Justification is God's free act whereby he declares the sinner in his courtroom standing in front him as "just" or "righteous." The sinner has grossly violated the law of God and deserves condemnation, but because of Christ's perfect obedience and substitutionary death, he is able not only to have his sins absolved and the penalty exonerated, he is also at the same time given a righteousness that qualifies him to exist within God's new covenant family. God's justification is a judicial declaration that is *not* based upon works of the law (Phil. 3:9; cf. Gal. 2:15-21), nor is it based upon a contribution of "goodness" from the totally depraved sinner. It is on the grounds of faith. It is *not* "infused" (the Roman Catholic view); it is imputed (the Reformed view). God does not look at the person and find some sort of spark of righteousness to *add* to the sinner, only to take it away if one commits a mortal sin. He gives it to the sinner on the grounds of faith alone and even then that faith is a gift from God.

These concepts are valuable because doctrine: (1) drives us to worship God and exalt him because of the remarkable truths found therein, and (2) motivates us unto obedience. As mentioned before, no command in Scripture is given without a truth behind it. And this next section is something Paul is going to hammer us with, and we will need these truths to navigate our way through it all.

THE TEXT
Paul cashes in his accountancy metaphor (pun intended) for an athletic one and begins with this:

> Not that I have already obtained this or am already perfect, but I press on to make it my own, because Christ Jesus has made me his own. Brothers, I do not consider that I have made it my own.[3]

Do me a favor. Put this book down and grab your iPhone/iPad or laptop computer and do a search on

---

[3] Phil. 3:12-13a

YouTube for the movie *Chariots of Fire*. If you have seen this movie before, then you know what I'm talking about. In this movie, there is a scene when Eric Liddell is pushed aside and falls down during a race (the 440 yard race back then). Liddell, instead of quitting in frustration, gets back on his feet and races past his opponents and wins the qualifying race. This scene is a perfect example of what I'm going to talk about in this section. Paul will draw on five different things that athletes do in order to illustrate for us what we must do as believers following Jesus.

At some point in our walk as Christians, we must have a holy *discontentment* (this is the first of five points). On one level, Christ is all-satisfying, and we don't have to look elsewhere. We should be content and satisfied in him. On another level, however, we cannot be idle with our pursuit of growth and sanctification. Yes, the objective reality of Christ's sufficiency and supremacy is ours in him; however, we are still called to take up our cross and follow him, and this requires us never to be content with just existing as followers of Jesus. We cannot be plateaued in our pursuit of holiness. It is always a fight to believe and a fight to enjoy God. His objectivity never changes, but our subjectivity and fight for joy sometimes does.

Paul unmistakably lays this out in these verses. He starts with the thought that he has not "obtained this." What is "this"? For Paul, he has just talked at length about Christ being his righteousness and how nothing in his past matters now because only Jesus stands in the "credit" column of the books. He says in 3:8-9a "[He has] suffered the loss of all things and count them as rubbish, in order that [he] may gain Christ and be found in him." Everything that Paul has worked for in his previous Pharisaical life is now dung. It counts for nothing because the only that that truly matters is gaining Christ and being found "in him." Paul's new-found identity is bound up with Christ himself. The "this" that Paul has not yet obtained he explains in 3:11. Paul desires to "attain the resurrection from the dead."

What does that mean?

For Paul, Christ has called him, given him a purpose, and now he must respond. At the end of this call is the resurrection of the dead. The Bible teaches that at the last trumpet, the dead will be resurrected, and those who are found in Christ will inherit the New Heavens and New Earth while those who rejected him will be told to depart, incurring the wrath of God in hell forever.[4] This is the goal for him. He wants to get resurrection life.

Paul has not yet attained this, and he is not content to sit around and wait. He wants to be fruitful. Because of 3:1-11, Paul can run with endurance. He knows that discipleship is a matter of constant growth and constant pursuit of Christ. What's at stake here for us is indifference and apathy. This is one of my greatest concerns as a pastor. Indifference will kill you. Never walk away from the Bible unmoved. There must be a holy discontentment in our lives. For Eric Liddell, he was

---

[4] See 1 Cor. 15; 1 Thess. 4:13-18; Mt. 7:23, 25:31-46; Rev. 21-22.

not content sitting there watching someone else win the race. He could have given up and stopped fighting in his exhaustion. But he didn't. He could have fought against the injustice of being pushed aside, but he didn't. He did not worry about other people, nor did he worry about the past—he saw the goal and was not satisfied until he got to the end. This is what Paul imagines here at the start of this section.

Another reason life is exhausting is because many believers think that their own moral effort is what is going to earn them God's favor. Trying to justify ourselves and make ourselves look good in front of others is exhausting. Inevitably, when running the race of life, we will commit two errors: (1) Thinking too much of ourselves, and (2) thinking too less of ourselves. Again, this goes back to identity. May we never be content with just cruising through life doing it all on our own. We must be found "in him."

The second thing Paul describes that fits the bill for both athletes and believers is *commitment.* He writes:

But one thing I do...[5]

"One thing," Paul says. One. Thing.

There is one mission (make disciples). There is one goal (resurrection). There is one savior (Jesus). There is only one commitment. For athletes, they specialize (usually) in one area. You do not typically have your

---

[5] Phil. 3:13b.

shot-put thrower run the 100 meter dash. You do not have your hockey team play soccer. Athletes commit themselves to one thing so that they can excel in it. If you've gone down the spiritual apathy trail, you have lost your focus. You have lost that one thing. Your vision is off kilter. You are unmoved by Jesus because you are being moved by other things.

For Liddell, he was dedicated to reaching the goal. There was one thing in his mind: getting to the finish line in front of the others. He could have stopped and quit running and tried something else. But that would have betrayed his purpose, for he was *good* at running. He had worked hard to do what he needed to do to be an excellent runner. He was *committed*.

This is a holy ambition. It is a sanctified fight for joy. It is a commitment to that one thing and never being satisfied or uncommitted to it until you have obtained it. Paul goes on:

> But one thing I do: forgetting what lies behind and straining forward to what lies ahead.[6]

Paul, like Liddell, looks at his past and forgets about it. In 3:1-11, Paul does this. He revisits his resume and sees it all as garbage because something of greater value has captured his life. Not only does Paul desire to forget the depraved things, he wants to forget the good things! Even his good righteousness pales in comparison to

---

[6] Phil. 3:13.

Christ. What Paul means by "forget" is that he is no longer going to be influenced by it. He is not going to let the past be a distraction on the way to the goal. To illustrate, it is similar to when God says he is going to forget our sin (Is. 43:25). It is not as though he has cosmic amnesia; no, God *doesn't hold it against us anymore.* Being committed to the goal means that we are no longer influenced by those past things. Jesus secures our identity, not our past.

A great question to ask is, "What has God done recently in your life as a tangible expression of his grace?" If you cannot answer this, you have plateaued and have not been committed to seeking his face. Commitment is a relentless pursuit of Jesus. Be stunned by him. Daily.

Not only is commitment necessary to Paul the athlete, *direction* is, too. He says that he is "staining forward." Theologians are divided on the exact visual Paul has in mind in the passage, because he could be talking about an ordinary foot race, or a chariot race. I tend to believe the arguments for a chariot race are a little more convincing, specifically because the word "straining" has its meaning in what a chariot racer would do to strain forward and hang on to the rope that binds the cart with the horse.

Nonetheless, Paul is moving forward. For Paul, it is not "go to heaven when you die" theology, though that is important. His entire argument rests upon 3:11 and the resurrection of the dead. This is what is ahead for him. Jesus is his goal, and he wants to attain resurrection life. Everyday Paul desires to be conformed to the image of Christ, to share in his sufferings (3:10) and journey towards this glorious future. For Christians, we tend to think of life in terms of "past, present, and future." We let the past dictate our present and future. What Paul seems to suggest, is that we are to let the future dictate our present and past. We cannot change the past, no doubt, but we can change its meaning. Again, when we "forget" the past, we are saying that we should not let it have negative influence on us *now* and in the future. We are to be citizens of heaven (next chapter), and because of this reality, we are forward looking people. To illustrate, you cannot run looking backwards. Try it some time. It's hard. You need to look forward to the goal to win, and you cannot look forward while looking backwards. Your past does not define you: Jesus does.

Paul goes on:

> I press on toward the goal for the prize of the upward call of God in Christ Jesus.[7]

The next athletic metaphor that we ought to unleash in our lives as we follow Jesus is *determination*. Paul says that he presses on. This word means to strive for, persevere, have concentration and conviction. Ultimately it is a call to be courageous. The Greek word finds its definition in hunting terms as it portrays someone chasing after his prey. To switch to the athletic

---

[7] Phil. 3:14.

metaphor again, what Paul is saying is that we do not win (reach the goal) by standing around watching. We get in the game and press on towards that goal by getting in the game. For many Christians, they are not in the game. They are idly standing by watching as spectators. In order to obtain this "upward call of God" (which in Paul's thinking is the resurrection life at the end), we must be active in our discipleship.

For Paul, he knows that each day brings new tasks to pursue courageously, and it requires a holy determination that is fueled by a passion for the supremacy of God in all things. Between the word of God taking root in our hearts and the Spirit's leading in our lives, we can press on with boldness and courage knowing that God is in it all.

This is also deeply connected to Paul's doctrine of justification by grace alone, through faith alone in Christ alone. One theologian said that:

> Trust in God's grace did not make Paul less active than the Judaizers but rather set him free now to run without watching his feet, without counting his steps, without competing with other servants of Christ.[8]

In other words, by banking on the promises of God in Christ, Paul didn't have to be a legalist. His self-righteousness is of no use anymore (3:1-11). His standing

---

[8] Ben Witherington, III, *Paul's Letter to the Philippians: A Socio-Rhetorical Commentary* (Grand Rapids, MI; Cambridge, U.K.: William B. Eerdmans Company, 2011). 208.

before God is not based upon his performance, or heritage—it is based upon Christ alone through faith alone. Keeping track of his steps and watching his feet is not going to help him get the goal. Striving forward will.

One of the ways that this plays out in contemporary theological practice in churches is the "let go and let God" motif. I think this is downright unhelpful. Would a quarterback ever get on the field and never listen to the coach? Worse yet, would he get on the field and never run a play expecting the coach to do it for him? At some level, yes, we need to cease striving and know that God is whom he says he is (Ps. 46:10). We need to let go of our control and let the Sovereign One do what he wants to do in and through us. But the "let go and let God" theology is not helpful and should never be used as an excuse for laziness in the Christian walk. Slipping into neutral and taking complete control without submission are both erroneous extremes.

Paul's determination is *synergistic*. In other words, it means that we have a duty to obey and follow Jesus, but left to ourselves, we cannot do it. We need a synthetic blend in our proverbial engines: our effort and duty coupled with the Spirit's work in our lives. Said differently, we are responsible for ourselves yet utterly dependent upon God to do anything (Phil. 2:12-13).

The final athletic metaphor that Paul gives us is *discipline*. He says:

> Let those of us who are mature think this way, and if in anything you think otherwise, God will reveal that also

to you. Only let us hold true to what we have attained.[9]

I bet that if I were to ask Michael Jordan about his athletic career and how he was able to do what he did, he would tell me that it required discipline. I don't think that he would tell me that he never had to work hard at basketball and that it just came naturally. I don't believe he would say that he never had to be disciplined. To the contrary, I bet he would tell me that discipline was at the root of it all.

What does it mean to be a disciple of Jesus? Certainly it means that we are following him. At its core, the word disciple means "learner." How can one learn without discipline? The two words are obviously related: discipleship requires discipline. And being disciplined is what it means to be a follower of Jesus.

In Paul's terminology, I think what he is saying in these verses is that you cannot just run the race: you have to obey the rules. There are certain things that are considered "out of bounds." The "anything goes" mentality is immature and has no place in the Christian walk. There is a reason that God demands us to be holy (Lev. 20:26; cf. 1 Pet. 1:16).

Being disciplined means being mature. Paul had already mentioned that he is not perfect (3:12), but he also says that if you think a certain way, you can be mature. In other words, we have what we need in Christ (3:1-11), but we are still called to run the race. The race

---

[9] Phil. 3:15-16.

has rules, and the race is still a race—there is still much work to be done even though we have it all in Christ. Maturity means running!

Look what Paul says in 1 Cor. 9:24-27:

> Do you not know that in a race all the runners run, but only one receives the prize? So run that you may obtain it. Every athlete exercises self-control in all things. They do it to receive a perishable wreath, but we an imperishable. So I do not run aimlessly; I do not box as one beating the air. But I discipline my body and keep it under control.

Do not run aimlessly. Do not be immature about this. Take it seriously. Be disciplined. Work hard knowing that God is at work. Like Liddell, get up, press on, and remain calm. Carry on. Run hard, even when you are tired. You do not have to count your steps nor do you need to worry about the others that are running. Hold on to what you have!

THE FIGHT FOR JOY WHEN YOU ARE TIRED

Discontentment, commitment, direction, determination, and discipline are all crucial elements to run well. However, it is truthfully exhausting. How can we do it?

> Therefore, since we are surrounded by so great a cloud of witnesses, let us also lay aside every weight, and sin that clings so closely, and let us run with endurance the race that is set before us, *looking to Jesus*, the founder and perfecter of our faith, who for the joy that was set before him endured the cross, despising the shame, and

is seated at the right hand of the throne of God.[10]

If there is ever any encouragement to be had in this exhausting race of life, the Bible gives it to us here. When I tell people to look to Jesus, what I am saying is, "Find yourself in desperate need and find his grace utterly sufficient." I think that is part of what the author of Hebrews is saying when he says "looking to Jesus." Since he is the founder and perfecter of our faith, we can look to him not only as an example, but a very present help in time of need (Ps. 46:1). We can run with endurance and look at Jesus and find him supremely satisfying. This is the fuel that keeps us fighting for joy when we are tired. *He* is the fuel!

No doubt people and things can rob us of joy. For the believer however, nothing can rob you of joy because Jesus is our joy and since we have him, nothing can sever it.

"Busy," says the man working two jobs in response to the question of how he is doing. It seems as if it will never end. But let's remember that this race is not a sprint. We are to press on, that is for sure, but let us pace ourselves. The Lord is patient with us, so we should endure. Are you tired? Find Jesus of ultimate worth and continue running. That's why it is called a "fight." It is a constant battle, one that requires diligence. But remember that we do not pursue holiness in order to get God's grace. We have God's grace so we can now pursue

---

[10] Heb. 12:1-2, emphasis mine.

it. To the downtrodden, sick, lonely and tired, I say, "Look to Jesus." His grace is truly sufficient. And now we wait for him.

JASON M. GARWOOD

9 - AS WE WAIT

Brothers, join in imitating me, and keep your eyes on those who walk according to the example you have in us. For many, of whom I have often told you and now tell you even with tears, walk as enemies of the cross of Christ. Their end is destruction, their god is their belly, and they glory in their shame, with minds set on earthly things. But our citizenship is in heaven, and from it we await a Savior, the Lord Jesus Christ, who will transform our lowly body to be like his glorious body, by the power that enables him even to subject all things to himself.[1]

Our culture has seemingly lost the virtue of delayed gratification. We live in a "buy now, pay later" world of instantaneous pleasure. At our fingertips lies the world and all of her promises of fulfillment. We are able to access gratifying pleasures at an ostensibly endless rate. When will it end?

---

[1] Phil. 3:17-21.

Never.

At least not any time soon.

It has been a problem ever since Eden.

I think back to when my parents first bought our family a computer. It was 1998, and the thing cost them about $1,600. At that time, I thought it was the coolest thing ever. I could get online and chat with my friends through *ICQ* and other online chat programs. I was able to get a *Hotmail* account and bypass the traditional snail-mail process. I was able to use the Internet to access information with our what-seemed-to-be-at-the-time lighting-fast dial-up connection. No longer did I need to do handwritten assignments. I was now able to print my homework in a professional manner.

Those were the days. The computer took our culture by storm as it made its way into our homes, providing us another layer of pleasure. Not only this, it captivated our attention, and we began to dream of what could be with technological advancement.

Today, my iPhone (in 2013) has more memory in it than that first computer could have ever dreamt about. It is astonishing how fast technology grows. Each year, a new product is unleashed that promises to better help our lives and circumstances. Because of the growth of communications, technology and the like, we can have these promises *now*.

Commercials do an exceptional job of trying to lure their customers in with special deals. "No interest for 5 years," they say. "Zero down, zero percent financing," says the car industry. It is everywhere. You can have all of the things you want *immediately*. Walk in empty handed, and you can leave with whatever you want. "No credit check required," is the doctrinal statement of our culture.

It is dangerous for several reasons.

The problem, I suppose, is that patience is now a lost art. I find myself blown away by the fact that I can have a one-year-old cell phone (that takes high-quality pictures, sends emails, posts tweets and fits in my pocket!) and find myself discontent when the newest one is announced. It's as if the one I have is complete garbage and might as well be a bag phone. Because of the culture I have sketched above, we are seeing the erosion of patience. Not only that, authentic satisfaction and contentment is hard to come by, too.

The ceiling of satisfaction is continuously reached. Trinkets and toys can only provide a certain amount of satisfaction before we move on to the next thing. It is what I was alluding to in the previous chapter with regards to idols. They are never fully satisfied; they continue to take from us without giving us anything in return. So we keep investing in them, hoping that somehow we can squeeze a bit of pleasure out of them, and when they run dry, we move on.

And on.

And on some more.

Is there something better? Is there *someone* better?

Indeed there is. The fight for joy is a fight to see and savor the infinite beauty and worth of Christ who will never, *ever* disappoint. Psalm 16:11 says, "You make known to me the path of life; in your presence there is fullness of joy; at your right hand are pleasures forevermore."

The tension we face in the here and now is that we are in the here and now and will be until Christ appears to restore all things. So what are we to do as we wait for him? How can we fight against the idols that over-promise in under-deliver? How can we refrain from the instant-gratification culture that surrounds us when we are called to contentment and a quiet life?[2] What is the task at hand while we wait? Paul tells us four things in this passage that can keep us from falling into the trap our culture has found itself in.

MAKE DISCIPLES

Many churches exist for many different reasons (so they think). Some exist to provide you with an entertaining experience. They will advertise themselves as having a live (and loud) rock band, a comedic experience with a funny pastor who loves to tell stories, along with a world-class cafe area with breathtaking coffee. They advertise these things, assuming the dead-in-sin rebellious sinner is going to find them appealing enough to come in and maybe hear the gospel (if it's even preached). Other churches flaunt themselves as being "for the outcast," believing that the mission of the church is social justice. Even still, others will engage with the poor, believing that righteousness is to be found living on the streets befriending the "least of these." While having a band and committing oneself to

---

[2] 1 Timothy 2:2.

social justice is *not* inherently unhealthy, it is not the mission of the church. There is only one mission given to us from our Lord. There is no other mission but this one:

> Now the eleven disciples went to Galilee, to the mountain which Jesus had directed them. And when they saw him they worshiped him, but some doubted. And Jesus came and said to them, "All authority in heaven and on earth has been given to me. Go therefore and make disciples of all nations, baptizing them in the name of the Father and of the Son and of the Holy Spirit, teaching them to observe all that I have commanded you. And behold, I am with you always, to the end of the age."[3]

Making disciples is the concern. You can do those things I outlined above, but do not mistake them for the central task of the church. Here's what Paul says:

> Brothers, join in imitating me, and keep your eyes on those who walk according to the example you have in us.[4]

Paul's entire life had been situated on Jesus and the task of making disciples. Nothing was able to side-track him from this incredible mission. In this verse, he writes to the Philippian church and encourages them to imitate

---

[3] Mt. 28:16-20.

[4] Phil. 3:17.

his life and "keep [their] eyes" affixed on those who are following Paul and his friends (Timothy being one example already praised in 2:19-24).

At first glance, this could seem incredibly arrogant. After all, Paul has said this elsewhere: "I urge you, then, be imitators of me" (1 Cor. 4:16). Part of the reason this is not arrogant is that Paul is urging the church to imitate Jesus in Paul, not Paul's shortcomings or sins. He wants to hold out to them his attitude towards Jesus and the pure and untarnished gospel message. Not only that, rabbinic Jews would have their students walk in their dust and do everything it is their rabbi would do. In this culture, discipleship happened in the front seat of life, not the back seat of a seminary. Teachers modeled for their students what they are to learn and do. This required an intimate relationship, one that can only be forged in the daily rhythms of life.

Discipleship for Paul is an invitation to join in on life, not just lecture. It is about participating in the daily grind of gospel ministry, not mere intellectual exercise. Instead of following those whose end is destruction (vs. 19), they are to follow godly examples and learn how it is to live a life that is fighting for joy centered on the gospel, treasuring in Jesus. Paul wanted them to see him repent just as much as exercise faith under duress. While only one verse, it packs a punch.

One of the modern errors of the church in disciple making is the belief that if people just get enough information about the Bible, they will become a better disciple. Think about it: why do we call it Sunday "school"? "School" implies information and information is all you get. Sure there is an element of fellowship, but it is not on mission in the world seeing lost people found. It is centered on getting more and more information about the Bible that is entirely devoid of missional incarnational living. This is the beauty of Paul's imitation invitation. It is about life, not mere knowledge transfer.

Another error in the modern world as it pertains to disciple making is the belief that a watered down approach to teaching is less offensive, and therefore, it will reach more people. In an effort to be "relevant" with the gospel, they leave the pure gospel behind. There are, of course, variations of this. Some altogether leave the gospel alone and never get to it because they do not believe it. Others dress it up on occasion, but it is not the driving force of the church. Moralism tends to be the fiber that runs through the church as people are told to "do better" rather than trust Jesus alone. "We don't want to offend people by talking about sin and repentance, so we just try to welcome them without judgment," they argue.

Wrong.

While *we* do not want to be a stumbling block to people becoming Christians, there is still a call to repent and believe, and the gospel itself is offensive as it is (Gal. 5:11; 1 Cor. 1:18-25). Our message is scandalous, and if we try and make it more palatable, we will lose that message. The Spirit changes people's hearts through the offense of the cross—let us stop fiddling with it and proclaim it!

The way discipleship is designed to work is in the

context of gospel communities on mission. These missional communities are pockets and groups of people who are living out their identity as a family of missional servants. They gather together to listen to the Spirit and creatively engage the world around them through gospel rhythms.[5] Rather than church being a time, place and location, (a concept foreign to the Bible), church is now an identity to be lived out in front of a watching world. If we are to imitate Christ, we are going to have to be willing to throw away the American dream and depend on the Spirit instead of our money. You cannot buy, manufacture or sell authentic gospel community. You can only depend on the Spirit of God to make disciples.

Furthermore, what Paul suggests is that we can also imitate other people who are following Jesus. This requires gospel community! It requires us to find someone to disciple (believer or not-yet believer) as well as find someone to disciple us. We are called to live our lives in such a way as to be worthy of the gospel (Phil. 1:27). It is a high calling, but we serve a gracious God. This is the first thing that we do when we fight for joy as we wait: make disciples. What else can we do?

WORSHIP TRUTHFULLY
The fight for joy is a fight to worship the Triune God truthfully. What I mean is we are to fight against

---

[5] For more on Gospel Rhythms, visit:
http://www.gcmcollective.org/article/soma-school-session-three-gospel-methods--everyday-gospel-rhythms/.

unbelief and wrong belief and fight for an accurate (true) understanding of the Godhead. Here's what Paul says next:

> For many, of whom I have often told you and not tell you even with tears, walk as enemies of the cross of Christ. Their end is destruction, their god is their belly, and they glory in their shame, with minds set on earthly things.[6]

Instead of imitating these aberrant teachers, Paul encourages his church to imitate those who follow Jesus. We do not know whom exactly these people are, but we know that it is not good.

Paul holds his character and approach to Christian ministry as an example to follow by saying that his end is resurrection life; his God is Jesus Christ, and his glory is found in God alone. Paul is running a race focused on the goal of getting God while this group is pacing slowly in life, focused on earthly things. For this group, presumably the Judaizers[7] (the Jews who said you had to be Jewish in order to be Christian), God is approached through food laws (making that your god), something Jesus clearly teaches against (Mk. 7:14-23). Consequently, their end is destruction. For Paul, this is blasphemous behavior in complete contradiction to the cross of Christ, thus making them true enemies. Their

---

[6] Phil. 3:18-19.

[7] You can read about this group in Galatians.

worship is not accurate, and because of it, they will be told "no" to entering the kingdom, no matter how good their works are (Mt. 7:21-23).

So how do we worship truthfully? Before I get into this a little further, it must be noted that Paul had already told the Philippian church to stay away from deceitful people once before. Now he reminds them again. Like Paul, we must warn people of false teachers and anyone who walks as an enemy of the gospel. But we must do so with tears. D.A. Carson clarifies for us:

> For our part, we must not become people who denounce but who do not weep. Neither may we become people who weep but who never denounce. Too much is at stake both ways.[8]

He is unquestionably right: Paul's heart is never simply to denounce a false teaching based on anger alone. He does it out of love as he warns the church yet again "even with tears." These false teachers must be avoided because their teaching is in direct contradiction to the gospel. What are some of the false teachings we are to avoid in order to worship truthfully?

I believe that Paul has in his mind a couple of different things that he wishes for us to stay away from. The reason I think this is so is because Paul has gone to enormous lengths to hold Jesus up, as well as get at the heart of our righteousness conundrum. This section is

---

[8] D.A. Carson, *Basics for Believers: An Exposition of Philippians* (Grand Rapids, MI: Baker Books, 1996), 93.

simply the fleshing out of what was put forth in 3:1-11.

The first warning is a false belief that we can be justified by death. In other words, many people hold to a universalism that says we can all go to heaven or succeed (however one defines it) in "the end" simply by dying. There is no ultimate truth out there, they say, but only the truth that we are all on the same journey towards the same destination. This is the view adopted by Oprah and many other "spiritual" people on television and the like. Paul combats this belief by holding up a vision of resurrection life that can only be obtained through justification by faith in Christ alone.

The second false belief is justification by church. This is the belief that attendance at a worship gathering and a kept-at-bay, loosely associated, come 30 times a year view of the church will get someone into heaven. It is the belief held up by the Roman Catholic Church that if you simply follow the rules and obey the various sacraments (and avoid mortal sins), then you can get to heaven. It is also the view that says you do not have to repent and believe, but must obey the church rules (and they are extensive!) in order to be declared righteous. Cults like the Jehovah's Witnesses and Mormons say that you cannot do anything without being in their group first. The problem is, according to Paul, is that you can only be saved by Jesus, not his bride or any other imposter of a bride. Even the bride needs saving!

The third issue at hand, and arguably the main one in the context of Philippians (and Romans and Galatians), is legalism: the belief that one can be justified by works. I have already talked about this at great length, so I will spare you the repetition. Paul believes that a sinner can be justified (declared right before a holy God) by grace alone through faith alone in Christ alone, and *not* through works of the law. The Judaizers are the prime candidates for this false view. They believed that Christ's atoning sacrifice was not enough for salvation and that followers of the Way must keep certain laws, like only eating certain things. These are "earthly things" as Paul puts it. They are not enough and cannot save. Only Jesus can. Ben Witherington helps us:

> Right standing with God was obtained by Christ's faithfulness and faith in Christ, and it is maintained by working out one's salvation with fear and trembling as God works in their midst to will and to do, following the examples of Christ and his servants. It is not worked out by adding Moses to Jesus, Moses' law to the law of Christ.[9]

This is how we worship truthfully. We own up to the full reality of whom Christ is and what he has done on our behalf. Any earthly, naturalistic explanation for salvation that leaves out the supernatural work of God the Holy Spirit does not communicate the biblical gospel. We worship in Spirit and Truth (Jn. 4:24), and the two go hand-in-hand. While we wait, there is another thing we can do, or better yet, remember.

---

[9] Ben Witherington, III, *Paul's Letter to the Philippians: A Socio-Rhetorical Commentary* (Grand Rapids, MI; Cambridge, U.K.: William B. Eerdmans Company, 2011). 215.

REMEMBER OUR CITIZENSHIP

In Jesus' time, Roman citizenship held significant privileges. Roman citizenship was one's identity as it was deeply connected to behavior in ethics (Acts 16:21) as well as one's allegiance to the empire and her cult. Citizenship gave a person certain rights that others did not have as well as provided a connection to the strongest empire in the known world. It provided protection and identity.

I mentioned in the first chapter some of the history behind the city of Philippi. After the civil war was over (see page 6), and rather than bringing thousands of soldiers back to the capital—which was already over-populated with a high unemployment rate—many of the Roman soldiers settled there and the city was declared a Roman colony. The city was deemed a legitimate Roman town even though it was outside of Italy. This brought added protection to the small colony as Rome would come to their rescue if invaded by a neighboring empire. Not only that, it provided Rome itself with an outpost of sorts that could act as a boundary marker for the growing (and complex) empire.

As the city settled, they awaited the time when the emperor would make his visit and appearance and celebrate with his people.[10] After all, the emperor was

---

[10] Whenever the emperor would visit a city, the people would come out and greet him and ceremonially usher him back into the city. This is clearly what Paul has in mind in the often misunderstood passage of 1 Thess. 4:13-18. In this passage, believers are "caught up" (resurrected) in the "air" (outside the city) to meet Christ who is coming down to restore all things (Second Coming).

worshiped as lord and savior and through the message of *Pax Romana* (peace of Rome), he was the bringer of good news.

With this in mind, Paul says:

> But our citizenship is in heaven, and from it we await a Savior, the Lord Jesus Christ.[11]

What Paul is trying to communicate to the Philippians, is that they are to have a different outlook, unlike those who look at earthly things. Not only are they to worship truthfully and make a confession that centers on the gospel, they are to remember and hold on to something that goes in direct contradiction and violation to their surrounding culture.

What Paul attempts to convey is *not* that we are to hope to die and go to heaven some day. He is not saying that the goal of the Christian life is to get to heaven. In fact, as I mentioned last chapter, Paul's end goal is *resurrection life*, which is life *after* life after death.[12] The Roman colony of Philippi would never just sit around hoping to go to Rome and live there someday as if its just supposed to happen to them.

No, what Roman citizens would do in their colony is bring the life of Rome to bear on their culture. Even if things got rough, they knew that the emperor and his

---

[11] Phil. 3:20.

[12] Thanks to N.T. Wright for first introducing me to this phrase and connotation.

royal army would come on their behalf and intervene to protect them. Bringing life to bear in their context meant cultivating the rhythms and practices of Rome in every facet of their culture.

Any Roman citizen would know exactly what Paul is hinting at here. She would know that there is a subtle yet powerful contradiction happening here—something that goes against the imperial cult.

Similar to the Roman people in Philippi, the church is a colony of the heavens whose task is to bring light to a dark and cold world. The church is not to sit around and hope to get zapped off of planet earth. Instead, we have a calling to cultivate the life to come in the here and now. This means that we pray for God's kingdom to come on earth as it is in heaven, anticipating the earth's renewal.[13] Philippi acted as an outpost of Rome; the church acts as an outpost of heaven.

For so long, Christians have gotten this backwards. They have taken the dualistic approach to the world and imposed it upon the faith. "The earth is bad," they purport, "so we must get out of here!" This is not the biblical vision of life on earth. Life on earth is a fight for joy in a God who, though in heaven, intends to bring his New Creation project to bear on his creation. This means that we fight for justice at the local level, advocating for the least of these who have no voice. This means making

---

[13] This means that we are to make, create, sustain, transform, impact and redeem certain aspects of culture. From business to farming, the Christian is to cultivate the beauty of creation in and through culture making.

disciples *through* serving those around us. The church is a finger pointing people to the kingdom of God. The church is a foretaste of the heavenly banquet to come. The church is a forerunner to the appearance of her savior. The church is a signpost of something greater and more marvelous than anything the world has to offer.

Where is *your* allegiance? So many American Christians have idolatrously confused this issue. They have held up the American ideal as being supreme instead of the kingdom of God as being supreme. This verse speaks volumes to us today who are witnessing a drastic change in American culture. No longer is Jesus the central focus at the town square. No longer is the church assumed to be the most influential group in a city. It is possible these days to talk with someone who has never heard of John 3:16, except for maybe seeing it at a football game on television. Christians are now learning what it means to live in a society where their views are not the predominant view. Culture wars and hotly contested political debates are fought in the name of Jesus.

We must take Paul's words here seriously and learn what it means to be a colony of heaven. Much like our culture today, Paul's audience does not see the Christian message as normative. We, too, are called to remember where our first and only allegiance lies: King Jesus. Paul reminds us of our citizenship not so we can escape from the earth some day, but so we can revel in the excellences of our majestic Lord.

Not only ought we to remember this, we are also

called to anticipate something with eager hope.

HOPE IN GOD AS WE WAIT
Paul continues:

> Who will transform our lowly body to be like his glorious body, by the power that enables him even to subject all things to himself.[14]

Paul's eschatological vision of the future centers on Jesus and what he has *already done*. This verse echoes 2:6-11 as Jesus is the blueprint for what will happen to us. Jesus' faithfulness to the Father led him to ultimate vindication and rescue. We, too, Paul says, will see the same future, pending we remember our citizenship and whom our true Lord is.

Paul says that when Christ appears, we will be "transformed" and given a new body—one that will never fade. Our resurrection future is secured by the same power that raised Jesus from the dead, the same power that created everything out of nothing. Because Jesus is Lord and has ultimate authority and power, he is subjecting all things to his rule and reign, and part of that subjection is the exaltation of his people.

How do we fight for joy as we wait? We hope in God.

At the center of this discussion is the sobering reminder that the call to follow Jesus is a real call. It is not a game. The fleeting pleasures of this world can and

---

[14] Phil. 3:21.

does choke the life out of someone who claims to be a believer. While waiting, many are drowning in the sea of their own idolatry, hopelessly indulging in "stuff." Some people think that it is hard to follow Jesus because it is too early to wake up on a Sunday and gather for worship.

If we are going to wait for this glorious appearance of our Lord, let us refrain from wasting our lives, nor find ourselves fooling around with drink and ambition. Let us be captivated by the beauty of Jesus and get to work.

10 - WHEN ANXIOUS

Therefore, my brothers, whom I love and long for, my joy and crown, stand firm thus in the Lord, my beloved. I entreat Euodia and I entreat Syntyche to agree in the Lord. Yes, I ask you also, true companion, help these women, who have labored side by side with me in the gospel together with Clement and the rest of my fellow workers, whose names are in the book of life. Rejoice in the Lord always; again I will say, rejoice. Let your reasonableness be known to everyone. The Lord is at hand; do not be anxious about anything, but in everything by prayer and supplication with thanksgiving let your requests be made known to God. And the peace of God, which surpasses all understanding, will guard your hearts and your minds in Christ Jesus. Finally, brothers, whatever is true, whatever is honorable, whatever is just, whatever is pure, whatever is lovely, whatever is commendable, if there is any excellence, if there is anything worthy of praise, think about these things. What you have learned and received and heard and seen in me—practice these things, and the God of peace will be with you.[1]

Anxiety is a troubling condition. It is one of the primary candidates for things that can rob us of joy. People can certainly rob us of joy, and many times they do, but the deep rooted anxiety we feel when *things* are out of our control is seemingly more devastating.

I remember one summer having some issues with anxiety. I was a full-time student, newly married and working a job I hated (but later had grown to love). I was stressed about several things and one night it had caught up to me. After having some chest pains, my wife took me to the emergency room. Back in high school, I had these same chest pains due to heart palpitations. Since then I have always had a fear of my heart suddenly stopping and me drifting off into eternity because of a heart attack.

Anyhow, while at the emergency room, they ran some tests and determined that my heart was taking a beating (my words, pun thoroughly intended) from the stress and anxiety in my life. Since I tend to internalize things, the natural result of that internalization was that my heart was hurting. I was told that my blood pressure was just fine and that nothing jumped out to them as being something of a concern. Apparently I just needed to relax.

Honestly, I understand it probably just as much, if

---

[1] Phil. 4:1-9.

not more, than the next person. I get the struggle with anxiety. It is horrible. It's horrible to internalize things so much so that a trip to the hospital is necessary. It is horrible to feel so much tension in your nerves that you feel like you could pass out. (Most of the time I will compensate for an over-stressed day by napping). But it is a real thing, and many a ulcers have been conceived because it.

The Greek word translated as "anxious" in Philippians 4:6 means "to be pulled in various directions." How fitting. Is this not a perfect visual? While hope is out in front of us, pulling us towards it, our fears and uncertainties yank us in the complete opposite direction. The crux of this thought process is the connection between belief and unbelief with regard to our past, present and future. It also has everything to do with our belief and unbelief in relation to what the gospel is and is not.

So how do we fight for joy when we are anxious? How can we look at the big picture of what God is doing in the world and find rest there? What are the things we need to know? What are the identities we need to reclaim? And what practices we can put into place in order to fight against anxiety and fight for joy in God? Ultimately there is no quick-fix solution to this. It is deeply connected to our faith and what we believe about God. It is also connected to prayer, and this is what Paul focuses on in this important section of the book.

STANDING FIRM
Having spent a considerable amount of time comparing

and contrasting his own view of the gospel against those who oppose him (1:15-18), as well as those who are enemies of the cross (3:18), Paul now appeals to the church to "stand firm." He writes,

> Therefore, my brothers, whom I love and long for, my joy and crown, *stand firm* thus in the Lord, my beloved.[2]

The entire book of Philippians is built around several central themes: joy, unity, Paul's affection for the church, the Trinity, Justification by grace alone through faith alone, Christ's humility and example, the Christian life, and the call to stand firm. While this is only one verse, it acts seamlessly as a segue into the next section as well as connecting it to what has come before.

Keep in mind what Paul has just done for three chapters.

In chapter 1, he has challenged the church to have a single-minded focus on the gospel. There are issues of partnership in the gospel (1-11), the expansion of the gospel (12-26), and the strong faith of the gospel (27-30) that must be kept as the central focus in our minds as we fight for joy.

In chapter 2, Paul challenges the church to be fully submitted to a focus on the gospel. They are to follow the examples of Christ (1-11), Paul (12-18), Timothy (19-24) and Epaphroditus (25-30) if they are to fight for joy and succeed in this battle.

---

[2] Phil. 4:1, emphasis mine.

In chapter 3, the church is to have a practical focus on the gospel. They do this by counting all things as a loss in order to get Christ who is of maximum significance (1-11). They also do this by pressing on, and moving forward (12-16) as well as awaiting their savior, the Lord Jesus (17-21). These elements, Paul says, help keep the practical focus of the gospel in front of our minds.

Finally, we arrive here in the final chapter of the book. Chapter 4 is about the security of the gospel and what it brings to the believer based upon who God is and what he does for the believer. Paul hones in on three crucial things about God: His peace (1-9), strength (10-13), and provision (14-23).

I made mention earlier in chapter 1 that I love the doctrinal insight that Paul brings to the table in this letter. I also love the practical focus on the Christian life and what it means to follow Jesus. Having said that, this section is significant in this way because it strikes at the heart of what it means to be a *unified* church.

Back in chapter 1 of Philippians Paul urges the church to live in light of gospel partnership and in doing so, their love will abound more and more. This is unity. He also says in chapter 1 that their lives should be lived only in such a way as to be worthy of the gospel and whether Paul is there or not, they are to stand firm (same phrase as our text here) in one spirit, with one mind, striving together for the faith of the gospel (vs. 27).

The theme of unity and standing firm together is brought up again in chapter 2. Paul desires for his joy to be completed by the church by being of the same mind, having the same love, and being in full accord, doing nothing out of rivalry and conceit, but instead, considering others as more important (2-4).

So what does it mean to stand firm (*steko*)?

The word is connected to perseverance. It means that we are to be constant and steadfast in our identities in Christ. We are not to diminish ourselves from our position in him. We are called to endure "in the Lord" by abiding in him (Jn. 15:4). We work, yes, but work and know that God is at work in us (Phil. 2:12-13).

Part of the reason that Paul says to stand firm is because of what he is about to address in the following verses. If anyone had reason to worry it was Paul! Facing division in Philippi, as well as the reality of his own impending death, Paul could have spent his life worrying, but instead chose to fight for joy. There are plenty of circumstances that will make us anxious. Against those things we will have to fight in order to obey Paul's command to stand firm. One of them is disunity.

DISUNITY
Paul continues:

> I entreat Euodia and I entreat Syntyche to agree in the Lord. Yes, I ask you also, true companion, help these women, who have labored side by side with me in the gospel together with Clement and the rest of my fellow

workers, whose names are in the book of life.[3]

The call to stand firm is not new to Paul. Jesus prayed in John 17:22-23 that the church would be "one," and "perfectly one." Paul had elsewhere talked about this issue, but here it seems that there has been an enormous disagreement between two key leaders in Philippi and Paul addresses it directly.

Apparently Euodia and Syntyche, two Christian women (their names are in the book of life!) had a falling out. There arose a disagreement and everyone knew about it (hence the reason Paul calls them by name). We do not know the extent of the disagreement, but it must have been severe, because Epaphroditus presumably told Paul about them when he arrived in Rome on his visit (see Phil. 2:25-30).

Whatever the disagreement—and it could have been something significant for they were leaders in the church—Paul urges them to stay united. It is intriguing that Paul does not say for them to humbly agree, but rather they are to agree "in the Lord." You can disagree with someone and still be unified. It is incredibly difficult, but this is what Paul had already communicated in 2:3 when he said, "do nothing out of rivalry or conceit, but in humility count others more significant than yourselves." He is not demanding that they agree with each other but that they agree in the Lord and stand firm (endure).

---

[3] Phil. 4:2-3.

Disunity in the local church is as commonplace today as it was back in Paul's day. In fact, the entire book of 1 Corinthians was written to correct a lot of pandemonium! There is a difference, however, between agreeing to disagree in unity, and just disagreeing. Two believers can still come together and be unified not because one compromises and the other stands strong, but because they can be unified under the commonality of Christ.

The call to stand firm is not a call to give up individuality or uniqueness (unity not uniformity!). It is a call to fight for joy *together*. Paul urges his "companion" (the Greek is *syzgos* and could be a proper name, though scholars disagree) to help them be unified. They are laborers in the gospel and have lost focus. Their names are in the book of life, but this companion (Epaphroditus?) is to be a mediator, helping them find a solution.

Unfortunately, there is much discord in the church today. Rather than confront issues directly, we passively ignore them. I get it. It is sometimes easier to let the "out of sight, out of mind" thing take over. And I've done it plenty of times before! But this is not Paul's position on the matter. He has labored hard over this letter, constantly revisiting this theme of unity because it is imperative for the gospel. Striving together means having the same mind and goal. For us, it is making disciples who make disciples, all of it centered on King Jesus and our gospel identities. If we lose sight of that common goal, then we will have disunity and that is a significant problem.

Disunity causes lot's of anxiety. One of the most frustrating things to do is confront someone with a concern you have. It has become normal to be passive aggressive instead of assertive. Because of this, we experience the gut-wrenching, pain-inducing feeling of anxiety. Unfortunately, we have a long way to go, but God is glorious and he alone is worthy to be feared (revered), so we do not have to fear other people.

It is difficult, however, to be unified. When you have different people, personalities and perspectives, you will naturally have some discord. Maybe someone said something on Facebook or wrote a nasty blog post about you. Maybe someone said something to someone else who heard it from someone else and then their hairstylist's neighbor's boyfriend's cousin brought it to you. Whatever the case, Jesus is Lord. He is our mediator and there is an abundance of hope readily available for us to indulge ourselves in.

When we fix our eyes on Jesus, any amount of discord or disagreement can be fixed. First we have to agree to move towards unity and also submit to the mediator who will call the shots. Jesus is our mediator. If Christ can reconcile us to God, we can be reconciled to each other by Jesus, too. And this is how Paul says it next:

Rejoice in the Lord always; again I will say, Rejoice.[4]

Think about it. What would you say to these two? Would

---

[4] Phil. 4:4.

you pull them into a room and let them share both sides to the story and then tell them just to get over it? What would you say to someone who is worrying? Get over it and move on? There has to be something else, and for Paul, it is the worship of the one true God.

The main theme of Philippians that we have focused on has been joy. It is compelling that Paul says here to "rejoice" (*chairo*) twice. The word means "to enjoy a state of happiness, well-being and joy." In other words, we enjoy the joy. We take delight in taking delight. The key, Paul says, is to take delight "in the Lord." Favorable circumstances will never give us joy because not every circumstance is favorable (it certainly wasn't for Euodia and Syntyche). Happiness is circumstantial and can be taken from you, but not joy in the Lord. Joy in the Lord cannot be taken because it is based on the immutable Glory of God found in Jesus. He never changes as Joy incarnate. Paul repeats this phrase because it is too good only to say once, and the key to being unified is the thing (or person) that we find unity *in*.

Both the object of our rejoicing and the timing of the act of rejoicing are essential. Paul says to do this "always." Not just on a Sunday morning. Always. At all times. No matter the occasion, we are commanded to rejoice. This is connected to the doctrine of Christian Hedonism. We are to be always fighting for joy in *God*. God is a happy God, and he loves happy Christians. Christians are those who are always rejoicing no matter the circumstance, time or place. Exalt him *always*.

THE FIGHT FOR JOY WHEN ANXIOUS

Discord between individuals can cause massive amounts of anxiety. We tend to fear what others think of us, and because of putting so much stock in what someone might think or say, we become distressed when the tension arises. This is the case in Philippi. Apparently the tension between these two women caused a ripple effect in the church and Paul is quick to offer some teaching. He does so by commanding them to rejoice,[5] and also gives them something to do. There are three things Paul encourages them to do, but before we get there, a word on 4:5.

> Let your reasonableness be known to everyone. The Lord is at hand.

Paul says that we are to be forbearing (this is what the word reasonableness means). We are to be gracious and gentle with everyone.

> The term "gentleness" was often used to describe an attitude of kindness where a normal response would be retaliation.[6]

When issues of discord and disunity arise, we are

---

[5] "Delight yourself in the Lord," is not a suggestion, but a command (Ps. 37:4).

[6] Clinton E. Arnold, *Zondervan Illustrated Bible Backgrounds Commentary Volume 3: Romans to Philemon.* (Grand Rapids, MI: Zondervan, 2002), 365.

instructed in those moments of testing to be gentle and forgiving rather than retaliatory. While joy may characterize our inward self, gentleness must characterize our outward actions when faced with difficult circumstances. This is crucial to remember when fighting against anxiety. When difficulties arise, our fight for joy is both in the heart and mind as well as in our hands. When anxiety comes we have both wrong feeling (heart) and wrong thinking (mind) and have the opportunity to fall into wrong acting (hands).

So why should we be gentle?

Because Jesus is coming. He is coming to judge both the righteous and the unrighteous. While here, the church is to be unified and we do this by striving together and being "reasonable" with everyone. In other words, the world is watching, and if we are to make disciples we need to fight against anxiety and fight for joy in God *in front of people*. We've been tasked with an incredible mission and some day that mission will be over when Jesus returns to restore all things. Knowing that he is coming provides added incentive for the Philippian church to continue the fight for joy by being characterized by forbearance.

Paul moves on in the fight for joy by talking about three things:

1. Gospel Prayer
2. Gospel Thinking
3. Gospel Living

He writes:

> Do not be anxious about anything, but in everything by prayer and supplication with thanksgiving let your requests be made known to God. And the peace of God which surpasses all understanding, will guard your hearts and your minds in Christ Jesus.[7]

Gospel prayer is the first tool we can use to fight for joy when we are anxious. In a culture of independence (we have a holiday named after it!), we hardly find ourselves in need, and ultimately this is what prayer is. Many of us do not pray because we do not think we are needy. But we are needy! We cannot control everything, and because of it we get anxious. Prayer, Paul says, centered on what God has done in Christ, is what we do to fight against anxiety.

When Jesus taught his disciples to pray, he said that they ought to pray for God's will to be done (Mt. 6:10). Anxiety, then, is our frustration about people and things that do not go our way, according to our will. We ought to pray for God's will to be done, not ours.

It is curious that Paul says not to worry about *anything*.[8] Nothing. Zilch. Nada. We are to seek God's kingdom first, remembering that being anxious adds nothing to our lives tomorrow, but only trouble for today. Not only that, he says we ought to pray about

---

[7] Phil. 4:6-7.

[8] See Jesus' remarks in Matthew 6:25-34.

everything. "Pray without ceasing," he tells us (1 Thess. 5:17). Usually we only think to pray when things are going wayward, but Paul says to do it all of the time. And we should. How often? Always. When? Always.

Keep in mind that Paul did not say, "just pray about it." I remember one time saying this exact thing to a friend's brother who was pouring his heart out to me. He was telling me all about how frustrating his life had become and how he hated what was happening to him. "Just pray about it, man," I said. What horrible advice![9] You see, for Paul it is never just prayer for the sake of prayer (meaning "rambling," the thing Jesus warned us about in Matthew 6:7). It is gospel prayer, and it involves three things: prayer, supplication, and thanksgiving.

The word *prayer* simply refers to the requests we make known to God. It involves worship and adoration as well as constant devotion to God. If we find ourselves worrying, our first action should be to close the door and pray (Mt. 6:8). When we do this, we commune with God and see his transcendent majesty. It is never only words said, but fellowship enjoyed. Usually we are quick to "vent" to God, when instead we ought to enjoy God in the midst of prayer. This is the first step in gospel prayer, an effort and desire to have time with him.

The second thing Paul says is *supplication.* This is the earnest fervor of our need. We are to pray like we mean it! Our Father wants to hear our prayer (Mt. 7:7-11), and

[9] Should we tell people to pray? Yes. But I did it in a nonchalant manner that was truthfully a cop-out answer because I did not want to listen to his concerns.

we do so with anticipation. This is the neediness we must cultivate. Neediness is absolute dependence on God. When we reject our own claims to self-sufficiency, this type of prayer makes us yearn for more of him (Ps. 42:1-4).

The third thing Paul says regarding our approach God with prayer is that we are to do so with *thanksgiving*. When praying, we express appreciation for whom God is and what he has done. It is our attitude of gratitude that triggers our prayers.[10] Oftentimes we are unappreciative of what God has done (most of the time we do not even notice it), and it shows in anxiety. Gratitude for what Jesus has done in his astonishing grace fuels the gospel-centered prayer.

Because we are quick to forget God's gifts and thank him for it, we become anxious. Not only that, we forget to pray about the little stuff in life. When we *assume* the gospel and God's grace in our lives, we *forget* all that he has done. The result of our gospel praying is that the "peace of God" guards the heart and mind. When anxiety strikes, we have wrong feelings and wrong thinking. But like a Roman soldier standing guard next to Paul, God's peace stands guard night and day, helping us realign ourselves towards the good news.

Think for a moment about the last time you were anxious. Was it an issue of wrong feelings, wrong belief or wrong actions? Was it an issue of feelings towards

---

[10] Even if we do not feel particularly grateful at the moment, it is still our duty to pray. Part of the fight for joy is continuing the duty while we wait for the delight to come.

someone or a situation, or was it something you *thought* about that had you stressed to the max? Maybe you did something you regret? Whatever the situation, when we pray, we activate God's peace and realign our false beliefs with the true beliefs about God and the gospel message. It is never enough to say to someone, "stop worrying." Worry is an issue of the heart and mind, not merely an external thing. The fight for joy when anxious is a fight to believe God and rest in his peace. Is this not the heart of the gospel? We were enemies of God, but Jesus stepped in our place and brought us peace? Our minds and hearts must be secured in the gospel truth of God's grace. And we get there through prayer.

Fighting for joy when anxious requires gospel prayer. But it also requires gospel thinking.

> Finally, brothers, whatever is true, whatever is honorable, what is just, whatever is pure, whatever is lovely, whatever is commendable, if there is any excellence, if there is anything worthy of praise, think about these things.[11]

If our minds are not renewed, our hearts will cling to untruth. If our hearts contemplate untruths, our minds will create worry. Welcome to the cycle of sin.

Paul says that we are to do some serious gospel thinking if we are to fight for joy when anxious.

Inside of our minds lies a battlefield. It is a war zone of temptation where we tend to believe things about

---

[11] Phil. 4:8.

idols that are really a lie. It is a battle between believing the false promises of sin and the true promises of God. Paul says in 2 Corinthians 10:5 that we are to, "take every thought captive to obey Christ."

In this section of Scripture, Paul gives us some things to think about—things that can help us fight against anxiety and take our deviant thoughts captive so we can obey Christ.

Whatever is true. Ever since the garden of Eden, man has loved evil and decided to believe that which is false (Rom. 1:25). Some of the things we worry about are legitimate issues. Some of them are not. Finding out what is true and what is not true is part of the battle in the mind. The Spirit leads us to truth (John 17:17; 1 John 5:6). We would do well to yield to the Spirit's work of drawing us to the gospel, the truth about God, and God's word. Thinking about what is true requires us to discern what is false.

Whatever is honorable and just. There are things that are right (just) and things that are worthy of respect (honor). Paul says that we are to think about these things. It is easy to think about things that are not right (because of sin) and things that are disrespectful (things of this world). The fight for joy when anxious is a fight to think about what is right and what is worthy of respect. We ought to be diligent in discerning what is what because sin will cloud our minds if we are not careful.[12]

Whatever is pure, lovely, and commendable. We live in a culture of impurity, unattractiveness and dishonor. Paul says to think about things that are pure, and by "pure," he most certainly means moral purity. We live in a highly sexualized culture and are frequently tempted to compromise our call to holiness. It starts with what we think about and put before our hearts and minds.[13] Fight against it. "Lovely," refers to things that are attractive and appealing. Think about beauty as God sees it, not as the world sees it. "Commendable" refers to those things that are worth looking at because they are good. These are godly things we must think about because they are oftentimes good gifts given to us by God. Rather than fill our minds with things of ill repute, we must focus on things that are commendable while throwing away the garbage.

Whatever possesses excellence and praise. "Excellence," refers to virtue (see 2 Pet. 1:5). These are the things that are honorable to God and fellow man. If

---

[12] I had a conversation at lunch recently with some friends of mine and I made mention of the fact that we as Christians have made sarcasm a more noble virtue than encouragement. Sarcasm has become more a part of our language than encouraging someone with the gospel. This is not right, nor is it respectable.

[13] This is part of the issue with pornography. It is neither pure, lovely or commendable. It starts with our attitude towards what it truly is (wicked). We can mortify the flesh by mortifying the object in question.

they are "worthy of praise," they are worthy of worshiping God with, because he deserves our worship as the one of ultimate worth, the giver of good gifts.

Through gospel thinking, we can continue the fight for joy when anxious as God gives us peace in our minds through the word of God (Ps. 19:7-9; 119:65). When we align our thoughts accordingly, we worship and exalt God appropriately as well as serve others faithfully.

So far, we have talked about the fight for joy when anxious as it pertains to gospel prayer and gospel thinking. Now we conclude this section by learning about gospel living.

> What you have learned and received and heard and seen in me—practice these things, and the God of peace will be with you.[14]

If we are to do gospel living we must understand the gospel, and Paul has gone to extensive lengths to help the Philippian church understand it (2:1-11; 3:1-11, specifically). At the center of it all, is what Jesus has done on our behalf. I have reiterated this before, but just as a reminder, whenever there is a command to *do something*, there is always a truth behind it. The truth about God is that he is the God of peace and that he is always with us, guarding our minds. We can either respond to this truth in faith, or unbelief. But the

---

[14] Phil. 4:9.

question is not whether or not we are to cultivate this through gospel living. We are.

The Philippian church has already been instructed to imitate Paul (3:17), as well as others (2:19-30). Even for us today, we are to do this. If we are to fight for joy when we are facing the complexities of anxiety, we are to "practice" the things that we have learned, heard and seen in Paul.

The word "practice" (*prasso*) here means "to perform repeatedly or habitually." In the Greek language it is something we do continually, not something we do once and then we are finished. We are to commit to the undertaking of gospel living by carrying on with what Paul has demonstrated for us. What has he demonstrated?

Paul exhibited what it meant to fight for joy in all circumstances. He learned how to be content. He learned how to suffer well for the gospel. He also learned how to sacrifice himself for the gospel as well as for others. He was a man who had a single focus (Jesus), single goal (resurrection life) and single affection (glory of God). He was determined to know nothing but Christ and him crucified (1 Cor. 2:2). He was entirely sold out to the mission of God in the world. This is what we can put into practice. No, Paul was not perfect. But his savior was perfect. Gospel living requires transparency, room for repentance. It also requires that we invite others into our lives as Paul did the Philippian church.

Gospel prayer, gospel thinking, and gospel living: these are the things we use to fight for joy when anxious. The promise is that the God of peace will be with us. So why worry?

JASON M. GARWOOD

11 - **BEING CONTENT WITHOUT RICHES**

I rejoiced in the Lord greatly that now at length you have revived your concern for me. You were indeed concerned for me, but you had no opportunity. Not that I am speaking of being in need, for I have learned in whatever situation I am to be content. I know how to be brought low, and I know how to abound. In any and every circumstance, I have learned the secret of facing plenty and hunger, abundance and need. I can do all things through him who strengthens me.

Yet it was kind of you to share my trouble. And you Philippians yourselves know that in the beginning of the gospel, when I left Macedonia, no church entered into partnership with me in giving and receiving, except you only. Even in Thessalonica you sent me help for my needs once and again. Not that I seek the gift, but I seek the fruit that increases to your credit. I have received full payment, and more. I am well supplied, having received from Epaphroditus the gifts you sent, a fragrant offering, a sacrifice acceptable and pleasing to God. And my God will supply every need of yours according to his riches in glory in Christ Jesus. To our God and Father be glory forever and ever. Amen.

Greet every saint in Christ Jesus. The brothers who are with me greet you. All the saints greet you, especially those of Caesar's household. The grace of the Lord Jesus Christ be with your spirit.[1]

When I initially taught this section I broke it up into two weeks. I preached the first sermon about contentment and made that the focus (vs. 10-13), whilst the second message was about riches and Paul's attitude toward them (vs. 14-23). For this part of the book, I decided to combine the two sections into one chapter as Paul certainly has one continual thought that ties the two together. We will start with the first one.

CONTENTMENT

The subject of contentment was just as much a concern in Paul's day as it is in our day. We give ourselves to abundant idolatry, and it centers around an insatiable appetite for pleasure born in our depravity. To clarify, seeking pleasure is not wrong in and of itself. We were created to do this. However, we were created to give ourselves to the pursuit of pleasure *in God*. This is what it means to be a Christian hedonist. It means that our fight for joy is a fight for pleasure in God and not in stuff. Followers of Jesus are pleasure-in-God seekers.

Conversely, our culture is driven by the pleasure-in-self tenet. There are doctrinal statements on our

---

[1] Phil. 4:10-23.

clothing, in our commercials, and in our tweets. (Still think that doctrine is not that critical?) We are inundated with opportunities every second of the day to indulge our senses. Not a moment goes by when you and I do not have a decision to make about where our pleasure is going to be positioned. Can we enjoy stuff? Certainly. Where do we draw the line? We will come back to this.

Other than during the Super Bowl (when we are acutely aware of them), have you noticed how advertisers have changed commercials over the years? Back in the day, companies would market their product based upon the function of the item. They would tell you the price and demonstrate it for you right then and there. Now-a-days, commercials have things in them that are entirely unrelated to the product itself. For instance, you could be watching a jeans commercial and not even know it is about jeans because it shows some guys playing football while telling an irrelevant story. You can also watch a couple on television argue over the remote and suddenly realize it is about rental cars (I am admittedly over- exaggerating the point, but you get what I am saying).

Our culture has played fast and loose with needs and wants, and we ought to pay close attention. We largely do not have a problem of wants; we have a problem of needs. We do not watch a commercial and suddenly want something like we did before (albeit this is true some of the time). Now our deficiency is that we need things we do not even want. My sister-in-law said to my brother once, "How many Apple products do you need?"

I jumped in, "As many as Apple makes." This is the newfound conundrum we find ourselves in.[2] We need stuff we do not even want. We buy things we do not need, and we do it all, someone has said, to impress people we do not even enjoy. It is a cycle of idolatry that has gripped our culture.

Since we have confused these two things, we now find ourselves at a turning point. *Are we going to be contented people in a world of discontentment?* This is the difficulty. As Christians following Jesus into the world, we are summoned to a life marked by contentment. Since we are called this, and our culture is unable to get past it, we are now at a crossroads. How can we be content when everything within us, and outside of us, is screaming for something else? How can we repent from the desire to accumulate more and instead get more of God? What is the secret to finding contentment? Read on.

The sovereign providence of God. Paul has just instructed the Philippian church to rejoice always (4:4); be reasonable with everyone (4:5); abstain from anxiety through gospel prayer (4:6-7), and do some serious gospel thinking (4:8) and gospel living (4:9). This next

---

[2] This is not an issue that revolves around Apple alone. However, Apple has been successful in this by creating products that make you feel as though you could not live without them. I think Steve Jobs once told someone that he does not make what people want; he instead makes products that people do not even know they need, and it works. I'm not sure how I could live without my iPad Mini [sarcasm].

section is a model of what it looks like to do gospel living in a world contaminated with discontentment.

> I rejoiced in the Lord greatly that now at length you have revived your concern for me. You were indeed concerned for me, but you had no opportunity.[3]

The first thing Paul does in order to fight for joy being content is trust in the sovereign providential work of God. This is implied as he speaks of the connection he has to the church and how God fittingly worked it all out for him to receive their gift.

It had been ten years since Paul arrived in Philippi, ten years since he had heard from his precious church. You can imagine the heartfelt anguish he had in his soul as he yearned for his friends (see 1:3-4, 7). As mentioned beforehand, Paul planted this church on his way through Asia as he headed northwest from Israel. The story of the beginnings of the church is found in Acts 16 (see chapter 1). Ten years later, Paul receives a visit from a friend named Epaphroditus who brought him a gift. This is the scenario Paul is talking about in this verse. His friends came through for him again. Presumably they brought him money, food and clothing, and it must have been quite a bit, for Epaphroditus made a long, dangerous trip to come find Paul in Rome (see. 2:25-30).

As Paul reflects on contentment, he rests in the truth

---

[3] Phil. 4:10.

that God is providentially working out all things for Paul's good (Rom. 8:28).

The Bible is rich in content with regard to the doctrine of God's sovereignty.[4] His sovereignty refers to his lordship, and when we speak of sovereignty, we should note that it is connected to providence. Providence contains three fundamental aspects: (1) Preservation; (2) Concurrence; and (3) Governance.[5] Preservation means that he keeps all things existing as he originally designed. Concurrence means that God cooperates with every action of his creation, directing and causing them to function as they do. Lastly, governance means that God has a purpose, and he directs and governs (oversees) all things so that they accomplish whatever it is he wishes.

Paul is in prison, lonely and chock-full of suffering. He is hungry and thirsty, but he is joyful. Why is he joyful? How can he be content? Because God is sovereignly orchestrating everything, including Paul's imprisonment to achieve his own providential ends. Said another way, God has not left Paul, nor has he forsaken him; in fact, God is using this for his glory. God can act through natural means, or supernatural means (we call these miracles). Either way, God is in control and is ordering everything in the universe to bring about our good. *Everything.*

---

[4] I addressed some of this in chapter 3.

[5] See Wayne Grudem, *Systematic Theology* (Grand Rapids, MI: Zondervan, 1994), 315-354.

How can you *not* rejoice in this? Contentment for Paul is attainable because God is on the throne. When you and I believe with our head, heart and hands that God is orchestrating everything for our good, contentment will not be of concern.

Paul says that he rejoiced in the Lord "greatly" because they were able to come through for him. Even if they would have never come to see him, Paul would be content. But the church was able to make it to see him. Notice that he does not heap guilt upon them for leaving him for a decade. He affirms that they did not have a chance to do this. Regardless of circumstances (we will discuss this momentarily), Paul trusted in the hand of God as he leveraged his situation for the gospel.

Satisfaction with little. The second thing that helped Paul fight for joy through being content was his capacity for satisfaction with only a little.

> Not that I am speaking of being in need, for I have learned in whatever situation I am to be content.[6]

In America, we value the bigger and better. We love to super-size the American dream by getting more money and more possessions. Larger homes, bigger SUV's, faster gadgets and higher credit card limits are common goals in our country. Does this honestly bring contentment?

---

[6] Phil. 4:11.

I mentioned in the introduction to this chapter that we do not only need what we want we need what we do not want, as well. We are immersed in plenty of opportunities to pleasure ourselves with paraphernalia. Is this how we achieve a state of contentment?

The reality is because God is providentially orchestrating all things we can conclude that all things (both in plenty and without much) are sufficient enough. If it is true that he does all things for his glory and our good, then it holds that whatever it is we have, with that we can be content. It is not an issue of how much but of Whom. Whatever situation Paul has found himself in he has learned to be content.

In comparison to today's standards, Paul was undoubtedly a poor man. He did not have much. Unless you were a high-level politician, or a lucky inheritor of money you did not have a lot. But this did not matter to Paul. He is content, even with little.

The Greek word used for content means "self-sufficient," or "to be satisfied." Paul says the same thing in 2 Corinthians 9:8. The word signifies independence from any type of need at any point in life. In other words, contentment means that you are sufficient from any desire for something else. The Stoics would say that one should refrain from caring about anything. If you do not care about anything, you will have contentment. To the contrary, this is not at all what Paul is saying. It is not as though we do not care, but our cares are affixed on Someone not something.

The world is built around discontentment; however, the Christian is fighting for a superior affection and joy in God, not the things of this world. Paul says that he is not speaking in need. He does not wish to make the Philippian church feel as though he should have received this gift years ago. Instead, he sets the tone by explaining that self-sufficiency is rooted in the Sufficient One. Again, the issue is not of wants, but of need. Paul needed that which only God could provide and for him, this was good enough.

Regardless of the gift, Paul is telling us that it is *not* about what we have and what we do not have. It is about being satisfied with the Satisfactory One. Even with little, Paul could rejoice and keep his joy.

Independence from circumstances. Happiness is circumstantial. It differs from joy significantly because joy is stable while happiness is unstable. Happiness changes from day-to-day; joy does not. Happiness can come and go, but joy lasts forever. If we are to fight for joy through being content, we had better figure this out.

Paul has already said that he can be satisfied with little and that ultimately, he trusts in the sovereign One. The reason he can is because he lives above his circumstances.

> I know how to be brought low, and I know how to abound. In any and every circumstance, I have learned the secret of facing plenty and hunger, abundance and need.[7]

---

[7] Phil. 4:12.

Despite circumstances Paul found the secret to contentment. The secret, he says, is learning how to live above any and all circumstances. He says that he knows how to be brought low (i.e., get along with humble means such as food, clothing, and other daily needs), and he knows how to prosper. The word for abound in the Greek means "to overflow." There are times of prosperity, and times of poverty.

The main problem that we face today is that we in the West live in the overflow, thinking we are living in scarcity. The stress of day-to-day money management pressures us into believing that we are poor.[8] The reason we play the comparative game is because we believe that satisfaction and contentment are based upon what we have or do not have. We look at our circumstances and compare them to other people and draw the conclusions that we are either rich or poor; this is not what Paul tells us to do. It is the complete opposite, in fact.

You see Paul lived in both worlds. He knew how to live with much and how to live with little. The phrase "facing plenty" could also be translated as "being full." The Greek word was used of feeding and fattening animals. In other words, Paul knew how to feast like a king and starve like a slave.

The secret is that no matter what happens, we can be content because circumstances do *not* dictate how we respond. Satisfaction is not found in what we have or do

---

[8] There are those in our own cities in America that are poor, but the average American is not when compared to the rest of the world.

not have. It is found in a superior joy, namely the Triune God of the universe. Paul was able to live above his circumstances. Living above circumstances requires our affections to terminate on God and nothing else. We must live independent of circumstances.

There is still one more secret to fighting for joy through being content.

Sustenance from God. Contrary to what you have been taught about this verse before, you cannot truly do all things. Here is the verse I am referring to:

I can do all things through him who strengthens me.[9]

You cannot do whatever you want. I cannot do whatever I want. If I wanted to try out for the NBA, I would not get a team. In fact, I would not even try out because I would much rather keep my dignity. For some reason, this verse has ended up on coffee cups, and other Christianized trinkets only to be used to try and motivate us to ace a test, win a game, or smugly put someone in their place for feeling insufficient to accomplish something. This is not what Paul is saying, and the context proves it.

Remember that Paul is speaking of contentment, and his secret is to trust a sovereign God, be satisfied with little and live independent from circumstances. Here, he implores us to live a life that is sustained by God.

---

[9] Phil. 4:13.

There is something spiritual behind the materialistic world. There is something more going on than the mere obtaining of stuff to fill our lives with a false sense of joy. All of it has to do with joy in God.

Let me start with what Paul is *not* saying. Paul is not saying that you can do whatever you please. He does not mean that he can do whatever he wants. (Do not forget that he is in prison. If all he meant was that he could do whatever he wanted, then I am sure he would not be in jail). Paul also is not saying that he can live without eating, sleeping or food and water. He needs the basics.

What Paul is getting at is that we are *not* self-sufficient, but Christ sufficient. Our sufficiency (contentment) comes from the Sufficient One. Behind all of Paul's rhetoric here is the ultimate truth that sustenance comes from God. Paul can "do all things," or better said, "endure all things," because Christ is working in him and he is providing him the strength to endure. When we come to the end of ourselves and our resources, we come to the beginning of God's resourceful sustenance. The bottom of human striving is the beginning of Godly strength. To translate it in a more helpful way, Paul says, "I am strong enough to endure everything that comes my way because Christ's strength is at work in me."

We are truly a discontented society. We are discontent with our jobs, marriages, schools, clothing, how we look, what we have and so on and so forth. The secret to contentment is not the absence of problems, for that will never happen. The secret is trusting in a sovereign God who gives us what we need, infuses his strength in us, grants us grace to live independent of circumstances, and promises to be with us always (Mt. 28:20b).

We are called to rejoice, always. We are told never to worry. We are promised that the peace of God will guard our hearts and minds. We are also guaranteed that the God of peace will be with us. All of this is learned. Paul says that he has learned the secret,[10] and it begins and ends with an immovable joy in Jesus. Do you believe it?

WITHOUT RICHES

This section is connected to the previous one as Paul fleshes out a bit more the topic of contentment. Here, he wraps up the letter of joy by expressing further thanks to the church for their gift.

> Yet it was kind of you to share my trouble. And you Philippians yourselves know that in the beginning of the gospel when I left Macedonia, no church entered into partnership with me in giving and receiving, except you only. Even in Thessalonica you sent me help for my needs once again.[11]

During Paul's travels, he would often work a job to pay

---

[10] The word "secret" that Paul uses in verse 12 is the same word used by those secret groups who held to themselves in privacy. Paul is saying that his secret is not private, but public and is accessible to all people everywhere. Like the initiation process for these secret groups, Paul sees his experiences of "highs and lows" as an initiation process for being content in Jesus.

[11] Phil. 4:14-16.

for basic needs and even then sometimes it did not go well. Often Paul depended on the graciousness of churches to help fund his travels, but even in doing so, he was reluctant to boast about it because he did not want the gospel to be seen as a pyramid scheme. Even still, the Philippian church remembers Paul and loves him to the point of bringing him some gifts.

After Paul left Philippi in Macedonia, he went to Thessalonica (Acts 17:1). Upon his arrival there, the Philippians helped him twice over (vs. 16). This is what spurred on Paul's writing of the letter of Philippians: he wants to thank them for the gift (vs. 14).

Paul says that they shared in his trouble. This is the heart of gospel partnership (see chapter 2). D.A. Carson reflects on these verses:

> In spite of what he says about this basic spiritual principle of dependence on God, Paul wants to affirm that he appreciated the kindness of the Philippians. It supported him in his *troubles*. He speaks of that time of 'the beginning of the gospel', words which have been understood in a variety of ways but which the NIV [New International Version} rightly takes as *the early days of your acquaintance with the gospel*. Paul had set out from Macedonia, the province in which Philippi was situated, and gone to Thessalonica (Acts 17:1). While he was there, the Philippian Christians *sent* him *aid again and again*. Notice also how he speaks of the partnership that existed between them, a sharing *in the matter of giving and receiving*. Real fellowship is a two-way

process.[12]

Paul's contentment is embedded in the belief that all he needs is God, and all he gets (good or bad) is from God, too. There is no need for Paul to accumulate stuff—he's grateful for whatever comes his way. Paul takes it a step further:

> Not that I seek the gift, but I seek the fruit that increases to your credit. I have received full payment, and more. I am well supplied, having received from Epaphroditus the gifts you sent, a fragrant offering, a sacrifice acceptable and pleasing to God. And my God will supply every need of yours according to his riches in glory in Christ Jesus. To our God and Father be glory forever and ever. Amen.[13]

While Paul affirms elsewhere that those who labor in gospel ministry ought to make their living by the gospel (1 Tim. 5:17-18; 2 Thess. 3:9-10; 1 Cor. 9:3-18), Paul never wishes to receive a gift to satisfy his own needs. He wants to return the credit (accountancy terms again) back to the Philippian church. Paul had already received so much help from his friends that he did not

---

[12] *New Bible Commentary: 21st Century Edition*, ed. D. A. Carson, R. T. France, J. A. Motyer and G. J. Wenham, 4th ed. (Leicester, England; Downers Grove, IL: Inter-Varsity Press, 1994). Php 4:10–20.

[13] Phil. 4:17-20.

want them to think that he was looking for more. He believed that he was "well supplied" and was able to get by just fine.

Part of the reason for Paul's attitude is because the gifts were a "fragrant offering, a sacrifice acceptable to God." In this phrase, Paul employs Old Testament language to prove his point. The term "fragrant offering" is used in Leviticus as an offering that pleases God (cf. Ex. 29:18; Ezek. 20:41; Jn. 12:3; 2 Cor. 2:16; Eph. 5:2). In other words, when Christians give, it brings immense blessing to those who are recipients of the gift, and God is pleased by it. Paul has been paid in full, so much so that he believes God will credit their gift right back into their account! Paul does not mean that we can earn stuff from God, as though God runs on the bartering system. No, Paul is grateful, content and knows that their gift is from God himself. He knew that their gift to him would result in God giving back to them what they need.

To be sure, God is no-one's debtor, and that everything we get is "according to his riches in glory in Christ Jesus." When God graces us, he graces us in accordance to our needs, not our wants. God knows exactly what we need, and this is why Paul is grateful. All of this to the glory of God. Forever and ever.

Paul's attitude in life was marked by a fight for joy being content without riches. He hints in verse 19 to the riches that are found in Christ Jesus. It is never enough for us to be content with what he have. We must be content with what we have *in Christ*. Paul did not wish to make a mockery of the self-giving gospel of Jesus by demanding more and more from the Philippians. They had done enough already; in fact, they had done more than enough. The reason Paul can say this is because he is content with whatever God brings his way! He did not desire more and more of stuff he desired more and more of God. This is the fight for joy: an insatiable hunger for God to be present right here, right now. Paul trusted the sovereign providence of God. He was content with little. He lived above his circumstances, and he knew that God would give him strength. The entire letter boils down to the gifts we receive in Christ.

Riches will die with us. The accumulation of wealth for the sake of this world does nothing for the world to come. The riches we need are found in Jesus, our only hope (Ps. 16:11).

> Greet every saint in Christ Jesus. The brothers who are with me greet you. All the saints greet you, especially those of Caesar's household. The grace of the Lord Jesus Christ be with your spirit.[14]

This is humbling. Even as I type this, I can sense the joy (and tears) in Paul's heart as he closes this masterfully written letter. He longs for his friends. He wants so much for them. He wants them to grow in grace. He alludes to "Caesar's household," and undoubtedly these are members of the elite in Rome who have met Jesus because of Paul's preaching. This reference must bring so much encouragement to the Philippians, knowing

---

[14] Phil. 21-23.

that the gospel has penetrated the highest ranks of the empire.

He calls them saints again. He sends his greetings, and then he asks that God's grace to be with them.

It is over.

The letter is finished. The entire Christian life begins and ends with the grace of our Lord Jesus Christ. I can imagine the look on their face when they read this aloud for the first time. Epaphroditus is back, and the apostle Paul sent them a letter. Such joy!

FINAL WORD

My prayer is that we would see a fight for joy unleashed in our churches. The fight for joy is not a single event; it is a lifestyle of work. As I was coming back from lunch today, I looked at the sign outside of our building. It reads, "Philippians: The Fight for Joy." As I read that, I prayed, "Lord, please let this never be just another series, just another book. Let this start a revolution." I asked God for this gift because I want nothing more than to see our church (and yours too) become single-minded, pleasure-in-God seekers. I want so badly to have the attitude of Paul in this letter. I want to know that if I go to jail, I will see it as gospel advancement. I want to know that if I receive a gift from someone, that I will be truly contented and that my prayer for the giver would be for God to credit their account. I want to rely heavily on my justification before God that has been given to me by Christ alone. I want to be intoxicated with the Spirit-anointed work of gospel partnership and gospel ministry. I want to pray without ceasing, believing that

God is at work in all circumstances. I want to fight for joy. I want Jesus.

I hope you do, too.

Let's get to work.

Soli Deo Gloria!

JASON M. GARWOOD

ABOUT THE AUTHOR

Jason M. Garwood (M.Div., Biblical Theological Seminary) is Lead Pastor of Colwood Church in Caro, MI. He and his wife have three children. You can connect with him online via twitter: @jasongarwood. He blogs at www.jasongarwood.com.

17912879R00122

Made in the USA
Charleston, SC
06 March 2013